Lecture Notes in Economics and Mathematical Systems

Managing Editors: M. Beckmann and W. Krelle

278

Walter E. Diewert

The Measurement of the Economic Benefits of Infrastructure Services

Springer-Verlag
Berlin Heidelberg New York London Paris Tokyo

Author

Prof. Walter E. Diewert
Department of Economics
University of British Columbia
Vancouver, B.C., Canada

ISBN 3-540-16810-9 Springer-Verlag Berlin Heidelberg New York
ISBN 0-387-16810-9 Springer-Verlag New York Berlin Heidelberg

Library of Congress Cataloging-in-Publication Data. Diewert, W. E. (W. Erwin) The measurement of the economic benefits of infrastructure services. (Lecture note in economics and mathematical system ; 278) Bibliography: p. 1. Infrastructure (Economics) I. Title. II. Series. HC79.C3D48 1986
363 86-22055
ISBN 3-540-16810-9
ISBN 0-387-16810-9 (U.S.)

Printing and binding: Druckhaus Beltz, Hemsbach/Bergstr.
2142/3140-543210

Preface

This research was supported by the World Bank and the Social Sciences and Humanities Research Council of Canada. Neither institution is responsible for the views expressed in this paper. The author is indebted to V. Corbo, A. Haymer, Y. Kanemoto, K. Lee, K. Mera, Hal Varian and A. Walters for helpful comments and to Elizabeth Lambert, Shehnaz Motani, and Jeanette Leigh Paisley for excellent typing services.

I would like to dedicate this book to my wife, Virginia.

TABLE OF CONTENTS

1. Introduction

A great deal of investment, both in developed and less developed countries, is made by governments and other public agencies in order to provide infrastructure services to consumers and producers in the affected region. The primary purpose of this report is to provide a methodology for evaluating the benefits (particularly to producers) of infrastructure investments.

It seems appropriate to list the types of infrastructure investment that we wish to model. The specific classes of investment we have in mind are grouped into the following four broader categories: utilities, communication, transportation and land development.

Utility Investments.

1. Water Supply.
2. Electricity Supply.
3. Natural Gas Supply.
4. Sewage Disposal.
5. Garbage Collection.

Communication Investments.

6. Telephone Services.
7. Postal Services.
8. Cable Services.

Transportation Investments.

9. Roads.
10. Railways.
11. The Construction of Airports.
12. Water: The Construction of Ports and Shipping Canals.

Land Development Projects.

13. Drainage Improvement Projects.

14. Flood Control Projects.

15. Irrigation Projects.

16. Pest Control Projects.

17. Erosion Control Projects.

18. Reforestation Projects.

19. Land Preparation Projects.

Most of the above categories of infrastructure improvement are self explanatory. With respect to categories 1 to 8, we mean that the relevant service is to be provided to an area which previously did not have access to that service. For most of these categories (garbage collection and the provision of postal services might be exceptions), bringing the service to the affected area is a major portion of the cost of providing that service. Typically, the additional cost of hooking up an extra household or business establishment to the area distribution network is low. Once an establishment is hooked up to the distribution network, the marginal cost of providing units of the service may be low (e.g., water supply, sewage disposal services) or relatively high (e.g., postal services, the supply of natural gas).

With respect to transportation investments, it is obvious that the provision of a new road (or an improvement made to an existing road) or the provision of a new rail link into an area will benefit businesses located in the area. Similarly, the construction or improvement of an airport or port will benefit consumers and producers in the surrounding area. It is less obvious but equally true that a transportation improvement made in one area will benefit even distant areas that are linked to the improving area. A similar comment applies to communication improvements. The fact that a tranportation or communication improvement may lead to benefits that are shared over a very large area complicates considerably the measurement of these benefits.

A few comments on the last general category of infrastructure improvements are in order. Drainage improvement projects could refer to the draining of swamps or they could refer to more pedestrian projects such as the provision of drains to carry away surplus rainfall. Flood control and irrigation projects are self explanatory. Pest control projects could refer to insect control or weed control. Erosion control and reforestation projects are self explanatory. Land preparation projects could refer to major inland sea reclamation projects (e.g., a Netherlands type project) or less exciting landfill or land clearing projects.

What virtually all of the above types of infrastructure investment projects have in common is that the provision of the service to an area provides benefits to many households and businesses in the area and it may be very difficult to charge users of the service the true marginal cost of providing that service (e.g., consider the case of roads). In the limiting case where all users have access to the infrastructure service at no charge, the service is called a <u>public good</u>. The majority of our 19 types of infrastructure investment projects are not pure public goods since access charges for the relevant service are frequently possible. However, these infrastructure projects are like public goods in at least two respects: (i) there is a substantial cost of providing the service to an area and a small marginal cost of adding an extra customer to the area service grid (in the pure public good case, the small marginal cost is zero) and (ii) charging customers the marginal cost of providing the service once the area service has been established will not lead to an efficient allocation of resources; i.e., marginal cost pricing won't work.

The reason why marginal cost pricing does not tend to work well in the context of pricing infrastructure services is the same reason why it does not work well in the context of providing the services of a pure public good: there is a problem in getting customers to reveal their true willingness to pay for the service. The pure public good case is explained well in Varian [1978;197-203]. The provision of infrastructure services case is similar. If the governmental authority asks households and business enterprises how much they would be willing to pay for an infrastructure service but the government tells these potential customers that it will not necessarily charge them according to their willingness to pay estimates, then these customers will have an incentive to inflate their willingness to pay estimates. On the other hand, if the government tells the potential customers that it will charge them for the service according to their willingness to pay bids, then the customers will have an incentive to deflate their willingness to pay estimates.

The above general discussion should make it clear that there are substantial theoretical and practical difficulties in measuring the contribution of infrastructure investments. Additional difficulties will become apparent as the reader works his way through this paper.

We conclude this section by providing a brief overview of the paper.

In Section 2, we introduce our first attempt at a measure of infrastructure benefits for a producer. The gross benefits to a producer in an area affected by an investment in infrastructure services are defined to be the producer's change in revenues minus variable costs (at constant reference prices for outputs and variable inputs). The two net revenues in the difference correspond to the pre and post project levels of infrastructure services. Any charges for the infrastructure services are excluded from these net revenues. We also hold constant the firm's initial endowment of land and fixed components of the capital stock. We find that the firm's restricted profit function is a useful tool which may be used to define the gross benefit measure in a succinct manner. A brief description of the properties of restricted profit functions may be found in Appendix 1. The net benefits of an infrastructure investment may be obtained by summing over the firm gross benefit measures in the project affected area and subtracting the cost of producing the infrastructure investment. We find that the government's cost function is a useful tool for describing the costs involved in producing the infrastructure investment. Appendix 2 describes briefly the relevant properties of cost functions.

In section 3, we explore the gross benefit function of an individual firm in the investment affected area in more detail. In particular, willingness to pay functions are introduced and are found to be derivatives of the firm's restricted profit function with respect to infrastructure variables. We show how integration of the areas under these willingness to pay functions yields the gross benefit measure.

In section 4, we show how the gross benefit measure can be approximated by using ex post data on prices and quantities. Obviously the analysis presented in this section is of limited use from the viewpoint of evaluating the benefits of a proposed infrastructure investment, but it may be of some use from the viewpoint of an ex post evaluation of a project.

In section 5, we consider some of the theoretical limitations of the net benefit measure proposed in section 2. In section 5.1, we indicate that the static benefit measures developed in the previous sections can be given a dynamic interpretation under certain assumptions. However, the assumptions are somewhat restrictive and the informational difficulties that we encounter in the dynamic case are very severe. In section 5.2, we address the problem of the existence of local goods. The problem here is that the infrastructure investment project may cause the prices of local goods and services to change in a systematic (i.e., endogenous) manner. In section 5.2, we adapt a productive efficiency approach to project evaluation to deal with the problem of endogenous prices. This approach has the advantage that it depends only on producer information. In section 5.3, we bring into our modelling not only the existence of local goods, but also the existence of potential consumer benefits due to the infrastructure project. Once consumers are brought into the picture, we must face up to the difficulty that the infrastructure project may alter the distribution of income and welfare in the affected area, and hence it is difficult to separate the efficiency effects of the project from the redistributive effects. Our method for focussing on the efficiency aspects of the infrastructure project is to use the methodology pioneered by Allais [1943][1977] and Debreu [1951][1954] to determine the efficiency effects of eliminating tax or monopoly distortions: we freeze the real income distribution in the economy at the preproject levels, introduce the project and ask if we can extract some resources out of the economy as a result of the project while meeting all relevant demand and supply constraints. This seems to be a natural efficiency measure for a project and we develop its properties in section 5.3.

Having dealt at length with the conceptual problems associated with measuring infrastructure investment benefits, in section 6 we turn our attention to alternative methods for measuring a firm's gross benefit function. The gross benefit function is defined in terms of the firm's restricted profit function, so we need techniques for measuring this last function or the associated willingness to pay functions. In section 6.1, we discuss the sample survey or questionnaire approach. In section 6.2, we summarize the ex post accounting approach based on section 4. In section 6.3, we discuss the engineering or programming approach. In sections 6.4 and 6.5, we discuss two general equilibrium approaches. In section 6.6, we discuss various econometric techniques in an introductory manner.

In the remaining sections of the paper, we explore the econometric approach to measurement in more detail. Section 7 considers the problems involved in choosing an appropriate functional form while section 8 considers the problems associated with measuring the basic price and quantity data that must be used in the econometric approach. Section 9 considers additional problems that the researcher will encounter with the econometric approach when working with time series data while section 10 considers some of the problems associated with working with cross section data.

Readers who are interested only in the conceptual foundations for measures of the benefits of infrastructure investments need only read sections 2 through 5. Empirically oriented readers, who wish to estimate econometrically either production functions or their dual restricted profit functions, need only read sections 7 through 10 and Appendix 1. In particular, section 7 discusses functional form considerations in some detail. Section 8 provides a relatively comprehensive but succinct discussion of the measurement and aggregation problems that the researcher will encounter in attempting to estimate econometrically a production, cost or profit function. This section may be read independently of the rest of the paper.

Section 11 concludes.

Proofs of various propositions are presented in technical appendix 4.

Finally, each section concludes with some notes on the literature, which provide some historical references and suggestions for further reading.

Notes

The concept of a public good is due to Samuelson [1964]. As we mentioned in the text, Varian [1978;197-203] provides an excellent introduction to public goods and the associated free rider problems. Varian also discusses a variant of the Groves [1976] incentive mechanism, which will induce customers to reveal their correct willingness to pay functions. A knowledge of the Mathematical Appendix in Varian will enable the reader of the present paper to follow the proofs in this paper.

Productive efficiency approaches to project evaluation (and the elimination of distortions) are pursued in Diewert [1983a][1983b]. An Allais-Debreu approach to project benefit measurement may be found in Diewert, Turunen and Woodland [1984], Kanemoto and Mera [1984] and Diewert [1984b].

2. A Simple Producer Benefit Measure

Consider a region in which there are a finite number (F say) of profit maximizing firms or enterprises that consume various amounts of government infrastructure services of the types listed in the previous section. We assume that there are three classes of goods in this regional economy. Class 1 consists of N goods which can be bought or sold by firms at the fixed positive prices $(p_1,p_2,...,p_N)$ which we denote by the price vector p. Firm f's net supply vector for these N goods is denoted by $x^f \equiv (x_1^f,x_2^f,...,x_N^f)$. If $x_n^f > 0$, then firm f is producing good n as an output, while if $x_n^f < 0$, then firm f is using $-x_n^f > 0$ units of good n as an input. The second class of goods is a class of I infrastructure services that are provided by all levels of government to the inhabitants of the region. Included in the list of infrastructure services are potential new services that might be provided by the government but are being provided at zero levels in the current period. Firm f's consumption of the ith type of infrastructure service is denoted by the nonnegative number $s_i^f \geq 0$ for i = 1,...,I and f = 1,...,F. The vector of infrastucture services utilized by firm f will be denoted by the nonnegative vector $s^f \equiv (s_1^f,s_2^f,..., s_I^f) \geq 0_I$ where 0_I denotes a vector of zeros of of dimension I. The firm may or may not be paying any user charges for the use of the infrastructure services. If all of the infrastructure services were pure public goods, then we would have $s^f = s$, for f = 1,...,F; i.e., each firm can consume the common amount of each of the I types of infrastructure services. However, in general, we will assume that each firm is utilizing a firm specific amount of water, electricity, natural gas, postal services, rail services, etc. The third class of goods is a class of J fixed capital stocks. Firm f's holdings of the jth type of structure, land, or other fixed capital stock component is denoted by the nonnegative number $k_j^f \geq 0$ for j = 1,2,...,J and F = 1,2,...,F. The vector of fixed capital stocks held by firm f is denoted by the nonnegative vector $k^f = (k_1^f, k_2^f, \ldots, k_J^f) \geq 0_J$.

We assume that the a priori technology set for firm f is a closed subset T^f of N + I + J dimensional space: if $(x^f, s^f, k^f) \equiv (x_1^f, \ldots, x_N^f, s_1^f, \ldots, s_I^f, k_1^f, \ldots, k_J^f)$ belongs to T^f (written as $(x^f, s^f, k^f) \in T^f$), then the net output vector x^f is producible given that the firm has at its disposal the vector s^f of government infrastructure services and the vector k^f of fixed capital stocks.

Given an infrastructure services vector s^f and a capital vector k^f and a positive vector of prices $p \gg 0_N$ for variable outputs and inputs, the profit maximizing enterprise f will want to choose a net supply vector x^f which will maximize variable profits $p \cdot x^f \equiv \Sigma_{n=1}^N p_n x_n^f$ subject to the constraints of its technology set; i.e., firm f will want to solve the following restricted profit maximization problem:

$$(1) \qquad \max_x \{p \cdot x : (x, s^f, k^f) \in T^f\} \equiv \pi^f(p, s^f, k^f)$$

where $p \cdot x$ signifies the inner product of the vectors p and x; i.e., $p \cdot x \equiv \Sigma_{n=1}^N p_n x_n$. Suppose x^f solves (1). Then we have defined the firm's <u>restricted profit function</u> π^f by $p \cdot x^f = \pi^f(p, s^f, k^f)$; i.e., the maximum variable profits of firm f are a function of the price vector p it faces for its outputs and variable inputs, the vector of infrastructure services s^f it has at its disposal and its historically given vector of fixed capital inputs k^f.

The mathematical properties of restricted profit functions are developed in Appendix 1. In the Appendix, the vector s^f, k^f is combined into the vector z.

If firm f faces the constant product and input prices p and has a fixed vector k^f of capital stocks at its disposal, then what benefits will accrue to the firm if the government changes the firm f infrastructure services vector from s^{f0} to s^{f1}? If we ignore any possible charges for infrastructure services, a natural measure of firm f's gross benefits from the change in infracture services, G^f say, is the change in the firm's variable profits; i.e., define G^f for $f = 1,2,\ldots,F$ by

$$(2) \qquad G^f(s^{f0},s^{f1},p,k^f) \equiv \pi^f(p,s^{f1},k^f) - \pi^f(p,s^{f0},k^f).$$

The benefits of the infrastructure change to firm f are called gross benefits because we do not net out any changes in user charges that may accompany the infrastructure change. The firm f gross benefit change is also a measure of gross benefits changes to society since it represents a change in the quantities of outputs produced by the firm minus the change in the variable inputs utilized by the firm, where all outputs and inputs are valued at the constant reference prices $(p_1,p_2,\ldots,p_N) \equiv p$. This benefit to society is a gross one because we have not yet substracted off the change in government costs that are associated with the change in infrastructure services that were provided to firm f.

Note that the firm f gross benefit change measure G^f defined by (2) depends on the two infrastructure service vectors s^{f0} and s^{f1}, the reference variable price vector p and the reference firm f capital stock vector k^f.

We now sum over the firm benefit change measures in order to define the regional gross benefit change measure due to a change in the government's provision of infrastructure services from s^{f0} to s^{f1} for firm f, $f = 1,\ldots,F$:

$$(3)\qquad G(s^{10},\ldots,s^{F0};s^{11},\ldots,s^{F1};p;k^{1},\ldots,k^{F})$$

$$\equiv \Sigma_{f=1}^{F}\, G^{f}(s^{f0},s^{f1},p,k^{f})$$

$$\equiv \Sigma_{f=1}^{F}\, \{\pi^{f}(p,s^{f1},k^{f}) - \pi^{f}(p,s^{f0},k^{f})\}.$$

In the gross benefit change measure G defined by (3), we hold constant the prices of variable outputs and inputs p and the fixed capital stock vectors k^f for each firm.

We now need to measure the change in the costs of providing the change in the infrastructure services. We assume that the government technology set for producing the firm specific infrastructure services T^0 is a closed subset of N + FI + J dimensional space. If the point $(x^0,s^1,s^2,\ldots,s^F,K^0)$ belongs to T^0, then the government has at its disposal the nonnegative vector of inputs of variable goods, $x^0 \equiv (x_1^0,\ldots,x_N^0) \geq 0_N$, the nonnegative vector of fixed government capital stocks, $k^0 \equiv (k_1^0,\ldots,k_J^0) \geq 0_J$ and can produce the vector of infrastructure services $s^f \equiv (s_1^f,\ldots,s_I^f) \geq 0_I$ for firm f for f = 1,2, ...,F.

Given the positive price vector $p \equiv (p_1,\ldots,p_N) \gg 0_N$ for variable goods and given its nonnegative vector of capital stocks $k^0 \equiv (k_1^0,\ldots,k_J^0) \geq 0_J$, an efficient government will want to minimize the variable cost of producing the vector of firm infrastructure services $(s^1,s^2,\ldots,s^F) \geq 0_{IF}$; i.e., the government will want to solve the following cost minimization problem:

$$(4)\qquad c(p,s^1,\ldots,s^F,k^0) \equiv \min_x \{p\cdot x : (x,s^1,\ldots,s^F,k^0) \in T^0\}.$$

Thus if $x^0 \geq 0_N$ solves (4), then we have defined the government's <u>restricted cost function</u> c by $c(p,s^1,\ldots, s^F,k^0) = p\cdot x^0 \equiv \Sigma^N_{n=1}p_n x^0_n$, the the minimized variable cost. This minimized variable cost is a function of the price vector p that the government faces for its variable inputs, the vector of infrastructure services that it is producing for the F firms in the region, $s^1,s^2,\ldots,s^F$, and the capital stock vector k^0 the government has at its disposal.

The mathematical properties of restricted cost functions are developed in Appendix 2.

We now define the <u>net benefits</u> of a government change in infrastructure services for firm f from s^{f0} to s^{f1} for $f = 1,\ldots,F$, holding constant the reference price vector for variable goods p and holding constant the fixed capital stock vectors for the government and all of the firms, $k^0,k^1,\ldots,k^F$ to be (3) minus the change in government variable costs, i.e., the <u>net benefits function</u> B is defined by:

(5) $$B(s^{10},\ldots,s^{F0};s^{11},\ldots,s^{F1};p,k^0,k^1,\ldots,k^F)$$
$$\equiv \Sigma^F_{f=1}\{\pi^f(p,s^{f1},k^f) - \pi^f(p,s^{f0},k^f)\}$$
$$-\{c(p,s^{11},\ldots,s^{F1},k^0) - c(p,s^{10},\ldots,s^{F0},k^0)\}.$$

Some of the deficiencies of our net benefits measure B will be discussed in section 5 below. However, a few comments on the role of the reference price vector p and the reference capital stock vectors $k^0,k^1,\ldots,k^F$ are in order. We are holding the prices of variable goods fixed because for now, we are assuming that the region under consideration is small and changes in the regional demand or supply for these goods will not affect the "world" prices. Thus we do not wish to contaminate the effects of changes in infrastructure service availabilities with the effects of exogenous changes in the region's terms of trade: we wish to focus on the pure efficiency effects of infrastructure investment projects. The government and firm capital stock vectors are held fixed because the region's endowment of natural resources, land and historically given capital stock components are fixed constraints.

Notice that the differences in the firm restricted profit functions, $\pi^f(p,s^{f1},k^f) - \pi^f(p,s^{f0},k^f)$, play a key role in definition (5). Thus in subsequent sections of this paper, we will focus our attention on methods for the empirical determination of these differences of the underlying profit functions π^f. Much of our discussion could be adapted to the analogous problems of estimating the difference in the government's restricted cost function, $c(p,s^{11},\ldots,s^{F1},k^0) - c(p,s^{10},\ldots,s^{F0},k^0)$. However, the assumption of cost minimizing behaviour on the part of the government may be harder to justify than the assumption of variable profit maximization on the part of firms.

Notes.

The mathematical properties of restricted profit and cost functions are discussed in Appendices 1 and 2, where the reader will find references to the literature.

Farrell [1957] suggested using differences in costs (and by extension, differences in profits) at constant reference prices to measure differences in efficiency between firms. In this section, we have adapted Farrell's idea by attributing an efficiency difference for the same firm to a difference in its utilization of infrastructure services. However, our suggested profit function measure of the direct benefits to a firm of a change in infrastructure services is explicit in Kanemoto [1980] who dealt with the pure public good case. The idea of using the sum of producer profits minus government costs as a "welfare" indicator for the entire production sector is due to Negishi [1972] and Harris [1978].

3. Willingness to Pay Functions and Marginal Cost Functions.

Recall that the gross measure of benefit change for firm f due to a change in infrastructure services from s^{f0} to s^{f1} was defined in the previous section to be the variable profit difference $\pi^f(p,s^{f1},k^f) - \pi^f(p,s^{f0},k^f)$. In this section, we explore this measure of firm benefit change in more detail. To save notational clutter, we shall drop the firm superscript f in what follows. Thus $\pi(p,s,k)$ refers to the restricted profit function for any one of the firms in our regional economy.

Let us temporarily further simplify the discussion by assuming that there is only one type of infrastructure service, so that I=1 and $s \geq 0$ is a scalar.

How much will the firm be willing to pay for an extra unit of infrastructure services given that it faces constant prices $(p_1,\ldots,p_N) \equiv p \gg 0_N$ for its outputs and variable inputs and has at its disposal the vector $k \equiv (k_1,\ldots,k_J) \geq 0_J$ of fixed capital stock components? A reasonable answer to this question for a profit maximizing firm would appear to be the additional profits that this extra unit of infrastructure services could generate; i.e.,

$$\text{(6)} \qquad \text{Marginal Gross Benefits} = \pi(p,s+1,k) - \pi(p,s,k).$$

If π is differentiable with respect to s, we can approximate the finite difference in (6) by the partial derivative $\partial\pi(p,s,k)/\partial s$. This derivative is defined to be the firm's <u>willingness to pay function</u> $w(p,s,k)$; i.e.,

(7) $$w(p,s,k) \equiv \partial\pi(p,s,k)/\partial s.$$

In the remainder of this section, we shall assume that π is differentiable with respect to s. We shall also assume that the underlying firm technology set T^f satisfies the free disposal property (5) in Appendix 1: this property simply means that extra units of s do not hurt the productivity of the firm. Under this assumption, we find that the willingness to pay function w defined by (7) above is nonnegative (see Proposition 2 in Appendix 1). A typical willingness to pay function might look something like the curve graphed in Figure 1 below.

Figure 1.

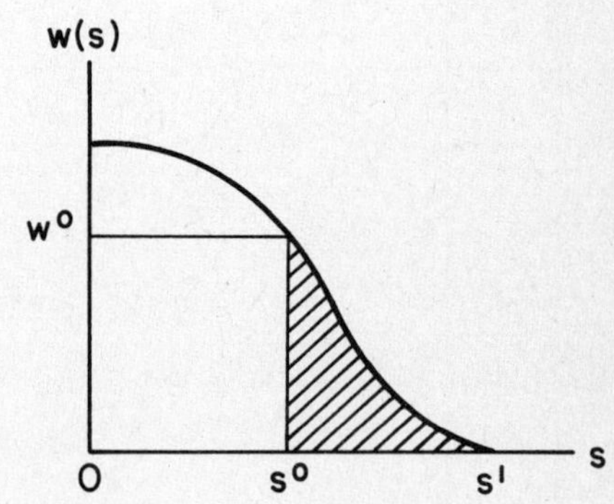

The willingness to pay function $w(s) \equiv \partial\pi(p,s,k)/\partial s$ function graphed in Figure 1 monotonically declines as s increases from 0 to s^1. Thus in this case, the curve is downward sloping; i.e., $w'(s) \equiv \partial^2\pi(p,s,,k)/\partial s^2 < 0$ for s between 0 and s^1. This case will occur if the underlying technology set T^f is a convex set (see Proposition 3 in Appendix 1 and the inequality (35) in this Appendix where $z_m \equiv s$). However, if T^f is not convex, then w(s) could be upward sloping.

From a theorem in elementary calculus, we can write the firm's change in gross benefits from the infrastructure change as the area under the willingness to pay function between s^0 and s^1; i.e., we have

$$(8) \qquad \pi(p,s^1,k) - \pi(p,s^0k) = \int_{s^0}^{s^1} [\partial\pi(p,s,k)/\partial s]ds$$

$$= \int_{s^0}^{s^1} w(p,s,k)ds \qquad \text{using (7).}$$

For example, in Figure 1, the firm's change in variable profits due to an expansion of infrastructure services from s^0 to s^1 (excluding any charges for the infrastructure services) is equal to the shaded area in Figure 1.

We now turn to the other side of the market and ask what it costs the government to supply extra unit of infrastructure services. Letting k^0 be the vector of government fixed capital stocks, the change in cost due to the provision of an extra unit of infrastructure services is obviously the cost difference $c(p,s+1,k^0) - c(p,s,k^0)$ where c is the restricted cost function defined in the previous section, except that we are now assuming that there is only one firm (so F=1) and only one infrastructure service (so I=1). Let us assume that $c(p,s,k^0)$ is differentiable with respect to s. Then the cost difference can be approximated by the partial derivative $\partial c(p,s,k^0)/\partial s$. This derivative is defined to be the government's marginal cost function, $m(p,s,k^0)$; i.e.,

$$(9) \qquad m(p,s,k^0) \equiv \partial c(p,s,k^0)/\partial s.$$

If the government technology set satisfies the free disposal property (5) in Appendix 2, then by Proposition 2 in that Appendix, $c(p,s,k^0)$ is nondecreasing in s, so $m(p,s,k^0) \geq 0$. A typical marginal cost function might look something like curve graphed in figure 2 below.

Figure 2.

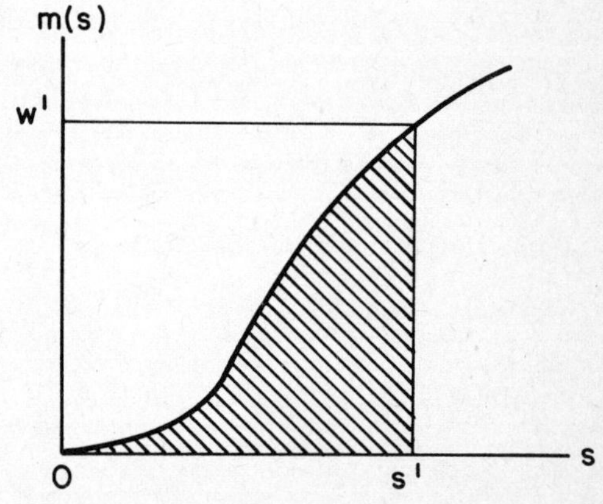

The marginal cost function $m(s) \equiv \partial c(p,s,k^0)/\partial s$ graphed in Figure 2 increases monotonically as s increases. Thus in this case, the curve is upward sloping; i.e., $m'(s) \equiv \partial^2 c(p,s,k^0)/\partial s^2 > 0$. This case will occur (or more precisely, the downward sloping case will not occur) if the underlying government technology set is a convex set (see Proposition 3 and the inequality (23) when I=1 in Appendix 2). The convex case rules out increasing returns to scale phenomena and thus is somewhat restrictive. In the general case, m(s) could be downward sloping, at least over an interval.

Again, using a theorem in elementary calculus, we can write the government's cost change due to a change in infrastructure supply to the single firm from s^0 to s^1 as the area under the marginal cost function between s^0 and s^1; i.e., we have

$$c(p,s^1k^0) - c(p,s^0k^0) = \int_{s^0}^{s^1} [\partial c(p,s,k^0)/\partial s]ds$$

(10) $$= \int_{s^0}^{s^1} m(p,s,k^0)ds \qquad \text{using (9).}$$

For example, in Figure 2, the government's increase in cost due to an expansion of infrastructure services from $s^0 = 0$ to s^1 (excluding any revenues received from the sale of infrastructure services) is the shaded area under the curve.

Consider the problem of maximizing the net benefits function $\pi(p,s,k) - c(p,s,k^0)$. Suppose the maximum is achieved at $s^1 > 0$. Since we have assumed that π and c are differentiable with respect to s, the following first order necessary condition will be satisfied:

(11) $$\partial\pi(p,s^1,k)/\partial s = \partial c(p,s^1,k)/\partial s \equiv w^1.$$

The algebraic condition (11) corresponds to a situation where the willingness to pay curve intersects the marginal cost curve at the <u>optimal user fee</u> w^1. Putting Figures 1 and 2 together yields Figure 3 below.

<u>Figure 3</u>

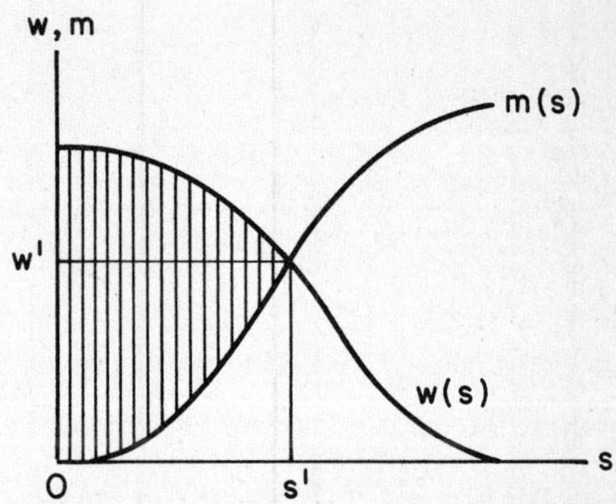

The shaded area in Figure 3 represents the area under the willingness to pay curve from 0 to s^1 (and this area represents the change in producer profits going from the $s^0 = 0$ situation to the s^1 situation) minus the area under the marginal cost curve from 0 to s^1 (and this area represents the change in government costs going from the $s^0 = 0$ situation to the s^1 situation). Thus the shaded area represents the net benefits function $B(0,s^1, p,k^0,k^1)$ defined by (5) when F=1, I=1 and s^0=0.

The shaded area in Figure 4 below represents the net benefits of a change in infrastructure services from an initial small positive level s^0 to a greater level s^2 which is less than the optimal level s^1.

Figure 4

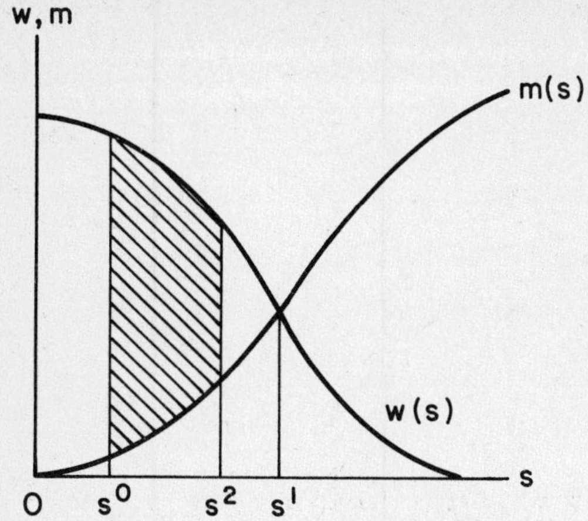

In Figure 5, the government's preproject level of infrastructure services is s^0 which is less than the optimal level s^1. However, we assume that the infrastructure investment project expands the supply of infrastructure services to the firm to the level s^3 which is greater than the optimal level. In this case, the net benefit change (5) can be represented by the shaded area to the left of s^1 minus the shaded area to the right of s^1.

Figure 5

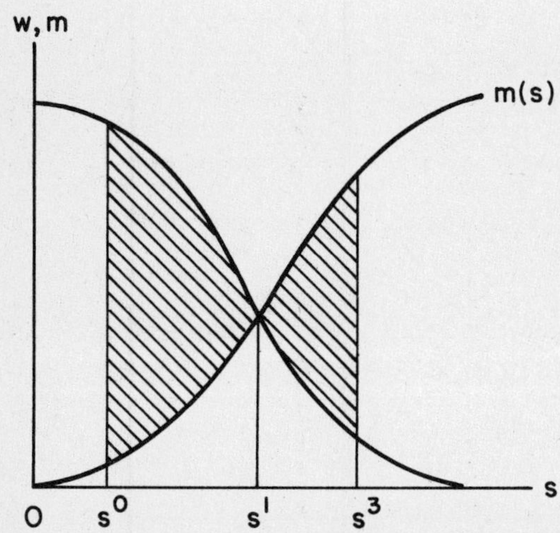

Let us now turn to the case where there is one firm and I infrastructure services that the government can supply to the firm. There will now be I willingness to pay functions, $w_i(p,s,k)$, $i = 1,2,\ldots,I$ where $s \equiv (s_1,\ldots,s_I)$ is now a vector of infrastructure services. In analogy to (7), the ith <u>willingness to pay function</u> is defined as the partial derivative of the variable profit function π with respect to s_i; i.e.,

$$w_i(p,s,k) \equiv \partial\pi(p,s,k)/\partial s_i, \qquad i = 1,\ldots,I. \tag{12}$$

The counterpart to (8) is now:

$$\begin{aligned}(13)\quad & \int_{s_1^0}^{s_1^1} w_1(p,s_1,s_2^0,s_3^0,\ldots,s_I^0,k)ds_1 + \int_{s_2^0}^{s_2^1} w_2(p,s_1^1,s_2,s_3^0,\ldots,s_I^0,k)ds_2 \\ & + \ldots + \int_{s_I^0}^{s_I^1} w_I(p,s_1^1,s_2^1,\ldots,s_{I-1}^1,s_I,k)ds_I \\ & = \int_{s_1^0}^{s_1^1} [\partial\pi(p,s_1,s_2^0,s_3^0,\ldots,s_I^0,k)/\partial s_1]ds_1 \\ & + \int_{s_2^0}^{s_2^1} [\partial\pi(p,s_1^1,s_2,s_3^0,\ldots,s_I^0,k)/\partial s_2]ds_2 + \ldots\end{aligned}$$

$$+ \int_{s_I^0}^{s_I^1} [\partial\pi(p,s_1^1,s_2^1,\ldots,s_{I-1}^1,s_I,k)/\partial s_I]ds_I \qquad \text{using (12)}$$

$$= \pi(p,s_1^1,s_2^0,s_3^0,\ldots s_I^0,k) - \pi(p,s_1^0,s_2^0,s_3^0,\ldots,s_I^0,k)$$

$$+ \pi(p,s_1^1,s_2^1,s_3^0,\ldots,s_I^0,k) - \pi(p,s_1^1,s_2^0,s_3^0,\ldots,s_I^0,k)$$

$$+ \ldots$$

$$+ \pi(p,s_1^1,s_2^1,\ldots,s_{I-1}^1,s_I^1,k) - \pi(p,s_1^1,s_2^1,\ldots,s_{I-1}^1,s_I^0,k)$$

$$= - \pi(p,s_1^0,s_2^0,s_3^0,\ldots,s_I^0,k) + \pi(p,s_1^1,s_2^1,\ldots,s_{I-1}^1,s_I^1,k)$$

upon cancelling terms

$$= \pi(p,s^1,k) - \pi(p,s^0,k)$$

where $s^1 \equiv (s_1^1,\ldots,s_I^1)$ and $s^0 \equiv (s_1^0,\ldots,s_I^0)$ are the post and preproject infrastructure service vectors utilized by the firm. Thus the firm's gross project benefits, $\pi(p,s^1,k) - \pi(p,s^0,k)$, can be obtained by integrating under each willingness to pay function in the manner defined by the first line of (13) and summing the resulting areas. Geometrically, we are summing I areas similar to the shaded area in Figure 1. The order in which we do the integrations in (13) is not crucial; i.e. instead of starting at $s^0 \equiv (s_1^0,s_2^0,\ldots,s_I^0)$ and integrating along the s_1 axis until we arrived at s_1^1, we could start at s^0 and integrate along the s_2 axis to arrive at $(s_1^0,s_2^1,s_3^0,\ldots,s_I^0)$ and then we could integrate along the s_1 axis to arrive at $(s_1^1,s_2^1,s_3^0,\ldots,s_I^0)$

and then do the remaining I-2 integrations in the same manner. We would still end up with the same answer, $\pi(p,s^1,k) - \pi(p,s^0,k)$.

(13) not only provides us with a nice geometric interpretation for our measure of firm gross benefits from the change in infrastructure services from s^0 to s^1, it also tells us that a knowledge of the firm's willingness to pay functions, $w_i(p,s,k)$, $i = 1,\ldots,I$, will enable us to evaluate the gross benefits measure.

The counterparts to our old univariate marginal cost function m defined by (9) are now the following I marginal cost functions, m_i:

$$(14) \qquad m_i(p,s,k^0) \equiv \partial c(p,s,k^0)/\partial s_i, \qquad 1 = 1,2,\ldots I,$$

where $c(p,s,k^0)$ is the government's restricted cost function and $s \equiv s_1,\ldots s_I)$.

It is straightforward to show that the following counterpart to the identity (13) is valid:

$$(15) \qquad c(p,s^1,k^0) - c(p,s^0,k^0) = \int_{s_1^0}^{s_1^1} m_1(p,s_1,s_2^0,s_3^0,\ldots,s_I^0,k^0)ds_1$$

$$+ \int_{s_2^0}^{s_2^1} m_2(p,s_1^1,s_2,s_3^0,\ldots,s_I^0,k^0)ds_2 + \ldots$$

$$+ \int_{s_I^0}^{s_I^1} m_I(p,s_1^1,s_2^1,\ldots,s_{I-1}^1,s_I,k^0)ds_I.$$

Thus the government's change in costs for providing a change in infrastructure services from s^0 to s^1 can be obtained by computing areas under the I marginal cost functions and then summing these areas. Hence a knowledge of the government's marginal cost functions $m_i(p,s,k^0)$ will enable us to evaluate this cost change.

We may subtract (15) from (13) and obtain an alternative expression for the net benefits function defined by (5) when the number of firms F=1. Geometrically, the resulting formula can be interpreted as a sum of I shaded areas similar to the shaded areas in Figure 4 above.

We turn now to a related topic and show that the willingness to pay functions defined by (12) can be interpreted as a system of firm (inverse) demand functions for infrastructure services under certain circumstances.

Let $p^* \gg 0_N$ be a given vector of variable goods prices, $s^* \geq 0_I$ a vector of infrastructure service utilizations by the firm and $k^* \geq 0_J$ a vector of fixed capital stocks for the firm. Suppose the firm's restricted profit function π is differentiable with respect to the components of s at the point p^*, s^*, k^* and define the nonnegative vector w^* as the vector of partial derivatives of π with respect to the components of s; i.e.,

$$(16) \qquad w^* \equiv \nabla_s \pi(p^*,s^*,k^*).$$

The vector equation (16) stands for the following I equations:

$$(17) \qquad \begin{aligned} w_1^* &\equiv \partial \pi(p^*,s^*,k^*)/\partial s_1 \\ &\vdots \\ w_I^* &\equiv \partial \pi(p^*,s^*,k^*)/\partial s_I. \end{aligned}$$

Suppose the firm were charged a user fee for each unit of the ith type of infrastructure service equal to w_i^* defined by (17) for $i = 1,2,\ldots,I$. Then a profit maximizing firm would demand a vector of infrastructure services which would solve the following profit maximization problem:

$$(18) \qquad \max_s \{\pi(p^*,s,k^*) - w^* \cdot s : s \geq 0_I\}$$

where $w^* \cdot s \equiv \Sigma_{i=1}^{I} w_i^* s_i$. Then using (16), it can be seen that s^* satisfies the first order necessary conditions for the maximization problem (18). It can be shown (in a manner analogous to the proof of Proposition 5 in Appendix 2) that s^* will in fact solve (18) if the firm's underlying technology set is convex. Thus under this convex technology assumption, the system of I willingness to pay functions defined by (12) may be interpreted as the firm's system of profit maximizing inverse demand functions for infrastructure services. Thus under the convexity assumption, the willingness to pay curve drawn in Figure 1 will be downward sloping (at least not upward sloping) and it may be interpreted as an ordinary demand curve for the infrastructure service.

Proposition 5 in Appendix 2 tells us that the following system of equations (19) defined in terms of the I marginal cost functions m_i defined by (14),

$$(19) \qquad w_i = m_i(p,s,k^0), \qquad i = 1,\ldots,I,$$

can be inverted to yield a system of government profit maximizing supply functions for the I types of infrastructure services, provided that the government technology set is convex. Thus the system of marginal cost functions may be interpreted as a system of inverse supply functions for infrastructure services, provided that the government technology set is convex.

It is worth emphasizing that the identities (13) and (15) are valid even if the private producer and government technology sets are not convex. The willingness to pay functions (12) and the marginal cost functions (14) are still well defined in the nonconvex case. However, the convexity assumption allows us to interpret the system of willingness to pay functions (12) as a system of (inverse) firm demand functions and the system of marginal cost functions (14) as a system of (inverse) government supply functions for infrastructure services.

We conclude this section by considering briefly the problem of maximizing the net benefits function (5) in the differentiable pure public good, many firm case. In this case, the same vector $s \geq 0_I$ of government supplied infrastructure services can be consumed by each of the F firms in the regional economy. The government's optimal provision of infrastructure services problem is:

$$(20) \qquad \max_s \{\Sigma_{f=1}^F \pi^f(p,s,k^f) - c(p,s,k^0) : s \geq 0_I\}.$$

Assume that $s^1 \gg 0_I$ solves (20). Then the following first order necessary conditions for (20) will be satisfied:

$$(21) \qquad \Sigma_{f=1}^F \nabla_s \pi^f(p,s^1,k^f) = \nabla_s c(p,s^1,k^0)$$

where $\nabla_s \pi^f(p,s^1,k^f)$ signifies the vector of first order partial derivatives of $\pi^f(p,s^1,k^f)$ with respect to the components of the s vector and $\nabla_s c(p,s^1,k^0)$ signifies the vector of first order partial derivatives of the government's restricted cost function c with respect to the components of s evaluated at (p,s^1,k^0).

The vector of optimal user fees w^f that the government should charge firm f for the use of infrastructure services is defined by

$$(22) \qquad w^f \equiv \nabla_s \pi^f(p,s^1,k^f), \qquad f = 1,2,\ldots,F.$$

Note that these fees will generally differ across firms.

The government's vector of marginal costs m^1 at the optimal production of infrastructure services is defined by

$$(23) \qquad m^1 \equiv \nabla_s c(p,s^1,k^0).$$

Now substitute (22) and (23) into (21) and we get $\Sigma_{f=1}^F w^f = m^1$.

The geometry of (21) can again be illustrated by Figure 3 if we assume I=1 and s^0=0. The w(s) curve in Figure 3 is now interpreted as the vertical sum of the individual firm curves, $w^f(s) \equiv \partial\pi^f(p,s,k^f)/\partial s$. The benefits are maximized at the point s^1 where $w(s) \equiv \Sigma_{f=1}^F w^f(s)$ crosses the marginal cost curve, m(s).

Notes

Diagrams similar to Figure 3 and 4 occur frequently in the producer and consumer surplus literature, which dates back to Dupuit [1844], Marshall [1920;811] and Hotelling [1938;243]. For more modern treatments, see Varian [1978;207-215] or Auerbach [1982]. However, all of the above treatments deal with situations where the interactions are between consumers and producers, rather than between producers and the government. Moreover, the above treatments assume that the willingness to pay functions and marginal cost functions are demand and supply functions respectively. As we have seen, this assumption is not required.

Both Varian [1978;214] and Auerbach [1982] identify producer's surplus as the level of profits a firm can make while supplying a certain quantity of output. We are adapting this idea to our present context; i.e., we are using the sum of producer profits minus government costs as a "welfare" indicator for the entire production sector.

Other than the work of Negishi [1972], Harris [1978] and Kanemoto [1980] referred to earlier, there does not appear to be a great deal of literature that is directly relevant to the problems studied in this section and the previous section. However, there are at least two strands of the economics literature that are indirectly relevant. The first is the planning literature which studies the optimal allocation of resources between production units; e.g., see Arrow [1964] and Heal [1969][1971]. The second is the literature on optimal transfer pricing: the <u>optimal user fee</u> defined by (11) above is analogous to the Hirshleifer [1956] Copithorne [1976] <u>efficient transfer price</u>. If the technology sets are convex, then the optimal user fee will also be a Hirshleifer [1956] <u>arm's length transfer price</u> or an Arrow [1964] decentralized profit maximizing transfer price. For a review of alternative concepts for transfer prices, see Diewert [1985a].

The pure public goods optimality conditions (21) are producer theory counterparts to some public good optimality conditions first obtained by Samuelson [1964] (see also Varian [1978;198] and Tsuneki [1984]).

4. Approximate Benefit Measures

Recall the net benefits function B defined by (5). The gross benefits of an infrastructure change from s^{fo} to s^{f1} for firm f were defined by (2) which we repeat below:

$$(24)\qquad G^f(p,s^{f0}, s^{f1}, k^f) \equiv \pi^f(p,s^{f1},k^f) - \pi^f(p,s^{f0},k^f),\ f = 1,\ldots,F$$

where π^f is firm f's restricted profit function defined by (1).

In this section, we shall study various first and second order approximations to the firm benefit measure (24). In order to simplify the notation, we shall drop the firm superscript f with the understanding that our analysis applies to any of the firms in our regional economy.

Let the data for the initial situation be $p^0 \equiv (p_1^0,\ldots,p_N^0)$, a positive price vector for variable goods; $x^0 \equiv (x_1^0,\ldots x_N^0)$, the corresponding net supply vector of the firm in period 0; $s^0 \equiv (s_1^0,\ldots.s_I^0)$, a nonnegative vector of infrastructure services that are being consumed by the firm in period 0, and $w^0 \equiv (w_0^1,\ldots,w_I^0)$ is the corresponding willingness to pay vector of the firm in period 0; i.e., $w_i^0 \equiv \partial\pi(p^0, s^0,k)/ds_i$ for i = 1,...,I where

$k \geq 0_J$ is the firm's vector of fixed capital stocks, (which will be held fixed in this section, and so we may write $\pi(p,s,k)$ more simply as $\pi(p,s)$ in what follows).

We assume that the government changes the firm's infrastructure vector to s^1 in period 1. We also allow for a change in the price vector for variable goods, so the new period 1 price vector is p^1 and the corresponding net supply vector is x^1. The firm's new willingness to pay vector is $w^1 \equiv (w_1^1,\ldots,w_I^1)$ where $w_i^1 = \partial\pi(p^1,s^1)/\partial s_i$ for $i = 1,\ldots,I$.

We may write the two willingness to pay vectors as gradient vectors (i.e., vectors of first order partial derivatives) of the profit function with respect to the components of s as follows:

$$(25) \qquad w^0 \equiv \nabla_s \pi(p^0,s^0); \; w^1 \equiv \nabla_s \pi(p^1,s^1).$$

Assuming that the producer maximizes variable profits in each period, we have the following equalities:

$$(26) \qquad \pi(p^0,s^0) = p^0 \cdot x^0 \equiv \Sigma_{n=1}^N p_n^0 x_n^0; \; \pi(p^1,s^1) = p^1 \cdot x^1 \equiv \Sigma_{n=1}^N p_n^1 x_n^1.$$

The variable profits $\pi(p^0,s^1)$ that the firm could earn if it faced prices p^0 and had infrastructure services s^1 at its disposal is not an observable number, but we may approximate it by means of a first order Taylor series approximation as follows:

$$(27) \qquad \pi(p^0,s^1) \simeq \pi(p^0,s^0) + \Sigma_{i=1}^I [\partial\pi(p^0,s^0)/\partial s_i][s_i^1 - s_i^0]$$

$$= p^0 \cdot x^0 \quad + \nabla_s \pi(p^0,s^0) \cdot (s^1-s^0) \qquad \text{using (26)}$$

$$= p^0 \cdot x^0 \quad + w^0 \cdot (s^1-s^0) \qquad \text{using (25).}$$

We may approximate the unobservable $\pi(p^1,s^0,)$ in a similar manner as follows:

(28) $$\pi(p^1,s^0) \simeq \pi(p^1,s^1) + \nabla_s \pi(p^1,s^1) \cdot (s^0-s^1)$$

$$= p^1 \cdot x^1 + w^1 \cdot (s^0-s^1) \qquad \text{using (25) and (26).}$$

Now substitute (27) and (28) into our gross benefits formula (24) and we obtain the approximate gross benefit measures (29) and (30):

$$G(p^0,s^0,s^1) \equiv \pi(p^0,s^1) - \pi(p^0,s^0)$$

$$\simeq p^0 \cdot x^0 + w^0 \cdot (s^1 - s^0) - p^0 \cdot x^0 \qquad \text{using (27)}$$

(29) $$= w^0 \cdot (s^1-s^0), \text{ and}$$

$$G(p^1,s^0,s^1) \equiv \pi(p^1,s^1) - \pi(p^1,s^0)$$

$$\simeq p^1 \cdot x^1 - [p^1 \cdot x^1 + w^1 \cdot (s^0-s^1)] \qquad \text{using (28)}$$

(30) $$= w^1 \cdot (s^1 - s^0)$$

The approximate benefit measure defined by (29) is perhaps more useful than (30). To numerically evaluate (29), we require information on s^0 (the initial vector of infrastructure services being consumed by the firm), the actual or proposed vector of services in period 1, s^1, and the vector of initial willingness to pay prices, w^0. Unfortunately, these prices may be difficult to observe, particularly for services being supplied at an initial zero level. On the positive side, if all services are being supplied initially at some user fee w_i^* for service i, then if the firm is maximizing profits, we can assume $w_i^0 = w_i^*$ for all i. The approximate benefit measure (30) is of course much harder to evaluate using just ex ante (i.e., period 0) data, since we need to know the firm's willingness to pay vector w^1 which will prevail at the proposed level of services s^1. However, from the viewpoint of ex post benefit measurement, (30) is no more difficult to evaluate than (29).

The above two ways for measuring the gross benefits to a firm of a change in infrastructure services are direct methods in the sense that we look directly at the markets for these infrastructure services. However, indirect methods for approximating the benefit measures defined by the left hand sides of (29) and (30) are also possible. A limitation of these indirect methods should be noted at the outset: they will only work if ex post data are available; i.e., we require price and quantity information for periods 0 and 1.

From equation (15) in Appendix 1 (Hotelling's Lemma), we have

$$(31) \qquad x^0 = \nabla_p \pi(p^0, s^0); \; x^1 = \nabla_p \pi(p^1, s^1);$$

i.e., assuming that π is differentiable with respect to the components of the price vector p, the period t net supply vector for variable goods x^t is equal to the vector of first order partial derivatives of $\pi(p^t, s^t)$ with respect to the components of p.

We use equations (31) to form the following first order Taylor series approximations:

$$\pi(p^0,s^1) \simeq \pi(p^1,s^1) + \nabla_p\pi(p^1,s^1)\cdot(p^0 - p^1)$$

$$= p^1\cdot x^1 + x^1\cdot(p^0 - p^1) \qquad \text{using (26) and (31)}$$

(32) $$= p^0\cdot x^1;$$

$$\pi(p^1,s^0) \simeq \pi(p^0,s^0) + \nabla_p\pi(p^0,s^0)\cdot(p^1 - p^0)$$

$$= p^0\cdot x^0 + x^0\cdot(p^1 - p^0) \qquad \text{using (26) and 31)}$$

(33) $$= p^1\cdot x^0.$$

Now we may obtain the following approximate gross benefit measures:

$$G(p^0,s^0,s^1) \equiv \pi(p^0,s^1) - \pi(p^0,s^0)$$

$$\simeq p^0\cdot x^1 - p^0\cdot x^0 \qquad \text{using (32) and (26)}$$

(34) $$= p^0\cdot(x^1 - x^0) \text{ and}$$

$$G(p^1,s^0,s^1) \equiv \pi(p^1,s^1) - \pi(p^1,s^0)$$

$$\simeq p^1\cdot x^1 - p^1\cdot x^0 \qquad \text{using (26) and (33)}$$

(35) $$= p^1\cdot(x^1 - x^0).$$

Note that (34) is the firm's net output change where all outputs and inputs are evaluated at period 0 prices, whereas (35) is the firm's net output change valued at period 1 prices. These approximate gross benefit measures aggregate nicely over firms, if all firms in the region face the same prices in each period. Aggregating (34) and (35) over firms leads to the following aggregate gross benefit measures:

$$(36)\qquad \Sigma_{f=1}^{F}\, p^{0}\cdot(x^{f1} - x^{f0}) = p^{0}\cdot\Sigma_{f=1}^{F}\, x^{f1} - p^{0}\cdot\Sigma_{f=1}^{F} x^{f0} \qquad \text{and}$$

$$(37)\qquad \Sigma_{f=1}^{F}\, p^{1}\cdot(x^{f1} - x^{f0}) = p^{1}\cdot\Sigma_{f=1}^{F} x^{f1} - p^{1}\cdot\, \Sigma_{f=1}^{F} x^{f0}.$$

Note that the measures (36) and (37) can be evaluated using only aggregate price and quantity data for the region. This is a definite advantage of the indirect methods for forming approximate gross benefit measures over the direct methods (29) and (30) discussed earlier.

Looking at the pair of direct benefit measures (29) and (30) and the pair of indirect measures (34) and (35), one might be tempted to form averages of the two pairs of measures in order to obtain a higher order approximation to an appropriate theoretical benefit measure. However, there is an obvious problem with such a suggestion. Suppose we took an average of (34) and (35) and formed the average benefit measure $(1/2)[p^0+p^1]\cdot[x^1-x^0]$. Then we could scale all of the prices in the period 1 price vector p^1 by a common positive scalar multiple, λ say, and x^1 would not be affected. But if we choose λ to be very small, our average benefit measure would approach 1/2 of the benefit measure defined by (34) and the contribution of (35) to the average would be negligible. This suggests that we shall have to take some care in taking averages of (29) and (30) or of (34) and (35).

Consider the following functional form for a firm's restricted profit function:

$$(38)\qquad \pi(p,s) \equiv g(p) + \Sigma_{i=1}^{I} s_i f_i(p) + (1/2)(\Sigma_{n=1}^{N} b_n p_n)(\Sigma_{i=1}^{I}\Sigma_{j=1}^{I}\, a_{ij} s_i s_j)$$

$$= g(p) + \Sigma_{i=1}^{I} s_i f_i(p) + (1/2)(b \cdot p)(s \cdot As)$$

where the functions $g(p)$ and $f_1(p)$, $f_2(p), \ldots, f_I(p)$ are linearly homogeneous, convex functions of p (see Appendix 1 for formal definitions of these concepts), $b > 0_N$ is a nonnegative, nonzero vector of fixed constants and A is an I by I symmetric matrix with elements a_{ij}.

Proposition 1: Suppose the firm's restricted profit function π is defined by (38) and the relations (25) and (26) hold. Then we have the following exact identity:

$$(39) \qquad (1/2)\{\pi(\tilde{p}^0,s^1) - \pi(\tilde{p}^0,s^0)\} + (1/2\{\pi(\tilde{p}^1,s^1) - \pi(\tilde{p}^1,s^0)\}$$
$$= (1/2)[\tilde{w}^0 + \tilde{w}^1]\cdot[s^1 - s^0],$$

where the normalized prices $\tilde{p}^t$ and $\tilde{w}^t$ are defined by

$$(40) \qquad \tilde{p}^t \equiv p^t/b\cdot p^t; \; \tilde{w}^t \equiv w^t/b\cdot p^t; \; t= 0,1.$$

A proof of Proposition 1 (and other Propositions in the main text) may be found in Appendix 4.

Note that the left hand side of (39) is an average of two theoretical firm gross benefit measures of the type defined by (24), whereas the right hand side is almost an average of our two first order approximate benefit measures defined by (29) and (30). We say almost, because the right hand side does not use the original willingness to pay vectors w^0 and w^1 defined by (25);

instead it uses the normalized willingness to pay vectors $\tilde{w}^0$ and $\tilde{w}^1$ defined by (40). Note that p^0 and w^0 are deflated by $b \cdot p^0 \equiv \Sigma_{n=1}^N b_n p_n^0$ where b is the nonnegative, nonzero vector which occurs in the definition of the restricted profit function (38). Similarly, p^1 and w^1 are deflated by $b \cdot p^1 \equiv \Sigma_{n=1}^N b_n p_n^1$ to form $\tilde{p}^1$ and $\tilde{w}^1$.

The significance of the class of functional forms defined by (38) is that this class can approximate an arbitrary twice continuously differentiable restricted profit function $\pi^*(p,s)$ to the second order; i.e., we have the following result:

<u>Proposition 2</u>: Let $p^* \gg 0_n$ and $s^* \geq 0_I$ and let a given restricted profit function π^* be twice continuously differentiable at (p^*,s^*). Then for any given nonnegative, nonzero vector $b > 0_N$, there exists a π in the class of functions defined by (38) (where the b which appears in (38) is the same as the given b) such that

(41) $$\pi(p^*,s^*) = \pi^*(p^*,s^*)$$

(42) $$\nabla_z \pi(p^*,s^*) = \nabla_z \pi^*(p^*,s^*) \qquad \text{where } z \equiv (p,s) \text{ and}$$

(43) $$\nabla_{zz}^2 \pi(p^*,s^*) = \nabla_{zz}^2 \pi^*(p^*,s^*);$$

i.e., the level, all N+I first order partial derivatives and all $(N+I)^2$ second order partial derivatives of π and π^* coincide at the point (p^*,s^*).

Putting Propositions 1 and 2 together, we obtain the following result: for any nonnegative, nonzero vector b, form the normalized prices $\tilde{w}^t$ defined by (40). Then $(1/2)[\tilde{w}^0 + \tilde{w}^1]\cdot[s^1 - s^0] \equiv (1/2)\Sigma_{i=1}^{I}(\tilde{w}_i^0 + \tilde{w}_i^1)(s_i^1 - s_i^0)$ will approximate the theoretical gross benefit measure on the left hand side of (39) to the <u>second</u> order. This is a very useful result.

The above results indicate that certain weighted averages of the first order benefit measures (29) and (30) do yield more acurate measures of benefits. Let us see if we can establish a similar accuracy result for a weighted average of the indirect first order benefit measures (34) and (35).

Consider the following functional form for a firm's restricted profit function $\pi(p,s)$:

$$\pi(p,s) \equiv \Sigma_{n=1}^{N} c_n p_n + (1/2)\Sigma_{m=1}^{N-1}\Sigma_{n=1}^{N-1} c_{mn} p_m p_n p_N^{-1} + \Sigma_{n=1}^{N} p_n g_n(s) \tag{44}$$

where the N-1 by N-1 matrix C which has elements c_{mn} for $m,n = 1,2,\ldots,N-1$ is symmetric and positive semidefinite and the functions $g_n(s)$, $n=1,\ldots,N$, are arbitrary functions of $s \equiv (s_1,\ldots,s_I)$.

<u>Proposition 3</u>: Suppose the firm's restricted profit function π is defined by (44) and the relations (26) and (31) hold. Then we have the following exact identity:

$$\begin{aligned}(1/2)\{\pi(p^0/p_N^0,s^1) - \pi(p^0/p_N^0,s^0)\} + (1/2)\{\pi(p^1/p_N^1,s^1) - \pi(p^1/p_N^1,s^0)\} \\ = (1/2)[(p^0/p_N^0) + (p^1/p_N^1)]\cdot[x^1 - x^0] \\ = (1/2)\Sigma_{n=1}^{N}[(p_n^0/p_N^0) + (p_n^1/p_N^1)][x_n^1 - x_n^0].\end{aligned} \tag{45}$$

Notice that the left hand side of (45) is an average of two theoretical firm gross benefit measures of the type defined by (24), whereas the right hand side is an average of the two first order approximate benefit measures (34) and (35) except that the price vector $p^0 \equiv (p_1^0,\ldots p_N^0)$ is replaced by the normalized price vector $p^0/p_N^0 \equiv (p_1^0/p_N^0,\ldots,p_{N-1}^0,/p_N^0,1)$ and the price vector p^1 is replaced by the price vector $p^1/p_N^1 \equiv (p_1^1/p_N^1,\ldots,p_{N-1}^1/p_N^1,1)$.

The class of functional forms defined by (44) can also approximate an arbitrary twice continuously differentiable restricted profit function $\pi^*(p,s)$ to the second order; i.e., we have the following result:

<u>Proposition 4</u>: Let $p^* \gg 0_N$ and $s^* \geq 0_I$ and let a given restricted profit function π^* be twice continuously differentiable at (p^*,s^*). Then there exists a π in the class of functions defined by (44) such that (41)-(43) hold.

Thus we may regard the right hand side of (45) as an approximate benefit measure which approximates the theoretical benefit measure which appears on the left hand side of (45) to the second order. This too is a very useful result. Our earlier comments on the nice aggregation properties of the benefit measures (34) and (35) also apply to (45).

<u>Notes</u>.

The first order approximation approach to benefit measurement (see (36) was pursued by Kanemoto [1980;139] in the context of a complete general equilibrium model. Revealed preference theory approaches to benefit measurement that use only pre and post project data have been developed by Negishi [1972] and Harris [1978].

The material presented in this section is related to the index number literature; see for example Caves, Christensen and Diewert [1982]. In this literature, the focus is on measuring ratios such as $\pi(p,s^1)/\pi(p,s^0)$ rather than differences such as $\pi(p,s^1) - \pi(p,s^0)$. However, the general principles are the same, particularly in terms of making empirically observable first order approximations and in relating certain "index number formulae", such as the right hand sides of (39) and (45), to flexible function forms. A functional form for $\pi(p,s)$ is "flexible" if equations (41)-(43) can be satisfied, so that π can provide a second order approximation to an arbitrary twice continuously differentiable function. The term "flexible" is due to Diewert [1974;113]. Following the index number literature (see Diewert [1976;117]), we might call the empirically implementable gross benefit measures on the right hand sides of (39) and (45) to be "superlative" formulae for the corresponding theoretical benefit measures on the left hand sides of (39) and (45), since they are exactly correct if the functional form for π is in the class defined by (38) and (44) respectively. Both of these latter classes of functional forms are flexible, as Propositions 2 and 4 demonstrate.

The idea that an average of two first order Taylor series approximations to a finite difference can provide a quadratic approximation to the difference can be found in Diewert [1976;118]. Quadratic approximations have a long history in applied welfare economics, dating back to Bowley [1928;224-225] at least.

The functional form defined by the first two sets of terms on the right hand side of (44), g(p) say, was utilized in Diewert and Wales [1984].

The approach to benefit measurement outlined in this section, which derived formulae involving price and quantity data that could be observed during the two periods under consideration, might be called the <u>accounting approach to benefit measurement</u>.

5. Problems with the Producer Benefit Measure.

5.1 Static versus Dynamic Benefit Measures.

Recall from definition (2) that the gross benefits of a change in infrastructure services for firm f from $s^{f0} \equiv (s_1^{f0},\ldots,s_I^{f0})$ to $s^{f1} \equiv (s_1^{f1},\ldots,s_I^{f1})$ was defined to be $\pi^f(p,s^{f1},k^f) - \pi^f(p,s^{f0},k^f)$, where π^f is the restricted profit function of firm f defined by (1) above, $p \gg 0_N$ is a reference vector of variable goods prices, and k^f is a reference vector of fixed capital stocks that the firm has at its disposal.

The gross benefit measure defined by (2) will almost certainly understate the benefits of the infrastructure change. The reason for this is that the change in infrastructure services from s^{f0} to s^{f1} will generally induce the firm to undertake longer term investment projects (that may take several years to complete) in order to take advantage of the services being provided by the new infrastructure service availabilities. For example, if a new electric power line has just been extended to a firm, it may pay the firm to replace its existing plant and equipment which ran on wood chips with new equipment which could utilize the electric power more effectively. Our static measure of gross benefits cannot capture this dynamic efficiency gain which was stimulated by the infrastructure change.

We may deal with these dynamic complications by extending our concept of the firm's production possibilities set T^f to be the set of outputs and inputs that can be produced and utilized over time, conditional on a time stream of infrastructure services that are being provided to the firm, and conditional on the firm's fixed capital stock vector k^f that the firm has inherited at the start of period 1. Thus we follow Hicks [1946;325-326], and assume that the firm's production possibilities set T^f is a set of vectors $(x^1,x^2,\ldots,x^T;s^{f1},s^{f2},\ldots,s^{fT};k^f)$, where $x^t \equiv (x_1^t,x_2^t,\ldots,x_N^t)$ represents the firm's planned production of outputs and utilization of inputs in period t (if $x_n^t < 0$, then good n is being used as an input in period t) for $t = 1,2,\ldots,T$; $s^{ft} \geq 0_I$ is the vector of infrastructure services that the firm expects will be made available to it during period t for $t = 1,\ldots,T.$; and $k^t \geq 0_J$ is the firm's starting capital stock vector that it has available at the beginning of period 1.

Let $p^t \equiv (p_1^t,p_2^t,\ldots,p_N^T) \gg 0_N$ be the positive vector of discounted period t prices that the firm expects to face in period t for $t = 1,\ldots,T$. We may now express the firm's intertemporal discounted profit maximization problem as follows:

$$(46)\qquad \max_{x^1,\ldots,x^T}\{\Sigma_{t=1}^T p^t\cdot x^t : (x^1,\ldots,x^T;s^{f1},\ldots,s^{fT};k^f) \in T^f\}$$

$$\equiv \pi^f(p^1,\ldots,p^T;s^{f1},\ldots,s^{fT};k^f)$$

and the maximization problem (46) serves to define the firm's intertemporal restricted profit function π^f, which has exactly the same properties as the static π^f defined by (1).

It would seem that all of our static theory could be adapted to the dynamic case if we used the π^f defined by (46) instead of the π^f defined by (2). For example, the old static gross benefits measure (2) would now be replaced by:

$$(47)\qquad G^f(s^{f10},\ldots,s^{fT0};s^{f11},\ldots,s^{fT1};p^1,\ldots,p^T;k^f)$$
$$\equiv \pi^f(p^1,\ldots,p^T;s^{f11},\ldots,s^{fT1};k^f) - \pi^f(p^1,\ldots,p^T;s^{f10},\ldots,s^{fT0},k^f).$$

The measure defined by (47) gives us the increase in the firm's discounted variable profits due to a change in the firm's intertemporal utilization stream of infrastructure services from $s^{f10},s^{f20},\ldots,s^{fT0}$ to s^{f11}, $s^{F21},\ldots,s^{fT1}$ at the constant reference prices $p^1,p^2,\ldots,p^T$ for variable goods. Thus the measure (47) also reflects the firm's change in net outputs at constant prices due to the change in the infrastructure service streams delivered to the firm.

We need to spell out in more detail what the components of the price vector $p^t \equiv (p_1^t,\ldots,p_N^t)$ might look like. If good n is an output, we would have

$$(48)\qquad p_n^t \equiv \tilde{p}_n^t/(1 + r_1)(1 + r_2)\ldots(1+r_{t-1})$$

where $\tilde{p}_n^t$ is the <u>selling</u> price for good n that firm f <u>expects</u> to prevail in period $t > 1$ (if $t = 1$, then $\tilde{p}_n^1$ is the observable market price for good n in the first period), and r_t is the interest rate that the firm faces in period t.

If good n is a nondurable input (i.e., the services of the input are completely used up during the period), then (48) will also suffice to define p_n^t, except that now $\tilde{p}_n^t$ is the spot <u>purchase</u> price for input n that the firm <u>expects</u> to face in period t.

If good n is a durable input (i.e., the input yields services over a number of periods rather than just during the purchase period), then the situation is more complex. Let $\tilde{p}_n^t$ denote the expected purchase price for one unit of a durable input n that will be purchased in period t and let $\tilde{P}_n^t$ denote the expected <u>scrap value</u> revenue the firm could expect to receive from selling one unit of the depreciated durable input in period T, the final period in our finite horizon model. Under these conditions, the price p_n^t is defined by

$$p_n^t \equiv [\tilde{p}_n^t/(1+r_1)(1+r_2)\ldots(1+r_{t-1})] - [\tilde{P}_n^t/(1+r_1)(1+r_2)\ldots(1+r_{T-1})] \,. \tag{49}$$

Formula (49) represents an intertemporal expected user cost for a unit of the nth durable input purchased in period t; it encorporates the usual interest rate and depreciation considerations that appear in more traditional user cost formulae. The user cost defined by (49) represents the net cost, discounted appropriately, of using the services of the durable input over the periods t,t+1,...,T in which it is expected to yield a stream of services. The final period scrap value price $\tilde{P}_n^t$ depends on t, the period in which a unit of good n is planned to be purchased, since the smaller t is, the greater will be the depreciation in the durable good, and so the smaller will be its expected scrap value, $\tilde{P}_n^t$.

The user cost formulae (49) assumes implicitly that the scrap value of a unit of durable input n purchased in period t is unaffected by the intensity of utilization of that good between periods t and T. If utilization effects are important, then they can be accomodated by increasing the dimensionality of our goods space NT. For example, planned purchases of durable good n in period t could be allocated into say three subclasses of goods which would correspond to the good being utilized intensively, lightly or at average levels over its lifetime. The definition and interpretation of the firm's technology set would be changed in accordance with this increase in dimensionality. Thus our model of intertemporal producer behavior is very general and could be modified to accomodate virtually any special model that the reader might suggest.

The government's static cost minimization problem (4) can be put into an intertemporal framework in a similar manner. To save on notation, we now define the firm f infrastructure services vector s^f to be the time stream of the period specific vectors s^{ft}; i.e., $s^f \equiv (s^{f1}, s^{f2}, \ldots, s^{fT})$ for f = $1,2,\ldots,F$. The government's intertemporal production possibilities set T^0 is now a set of vectors $(x^1, x^2, \ldots, x^T; s^1, s^2, \ldots, s^F; k^0)$ where $x^t \equiv (x_1^t, \ldots x_N^t) \geq 0_N$ represents the government's planned utilization of inputs during period t, the intertemporal firm infrastructure supply vectors $s^f \geq 0_{IT}$ have been defined above, and $k^0 \geq 0_J$ is the government's initial capital stock vector. The government's intertemporal cost minimization problem is:

$$\text{(50)} \qquad \min_{x^1,\ldots,x^T}\{\Sigma_{t=1}^T p^t \cdot x^t : (x^1,\ldots,x^T; s^1,\ldots,s^F; k^0) \in T\} \equiv c(p^1,\ldots,p^T; s^1,\ldots s^F; k^0)$$

where $p^t \equiv (p_1^t,\ldots,p_N^t) \gg 0_N$ for $t = 1,\ldots,T$ and the government's expected period t price for input n discounted to the present, p_n^t, is defined by (48) or (49) if the input is a durable good. Note that we have used the optimized objective function for the intertemporal cost minimization problem to define the government's _intertemporal restricted cost function_, c.

The intertemporal cost function defined by (50) will have the same mathematical properties as the static cost function defined (4), so there is no need to review these properties.

Our old _net benefits function_ B defined above by (5) can be extended to the intertemporal context: define $p \equiv (p^1,\ldots,p^T)$, replace the static profit functions π^f in (5) by their dynamic counterparts defined by (46) (where s^{f1}, $s^{f2},\ldots,s^{fT})$ is now defined to be s^f), and replace the static cost function c by its dynamic counterpart (50).

Thus it would appear that all of our static theory can readily be extended to the dynamic context. However, appearances can be deceptive.

The major problem in extending the static theory to the dynamic case is that the expected future discounted price vectors $p^2,p^3,\ldots,p^T$ are no longer observable market prices. From the viewpoint of ex ante analysis, we, as external observers, simply have no way of knowing what the expectations of firms and governments are about future prices. Even more troublesome is the problem of determining what the _solutions_ would be to the intertemporal profit maximization problems (46) and the intertemporal cost minimization problem (50). Without a knowledge of these solutions, we cannot even evaluate the ex ante gross benefit measure (29), let alone the ex post approximate measures (30), (34), (35), (39) and (45).

A less fundamental but still troublesome problem with our dynamic extension of the static theory is that our intertemporal interpretation of the net benefits function (5) implicitly assumes that all firms and the government face the same sequence of one period interest rates r_t or opportunity costs of capital. This is an extremely unlikely occurance.

A final difficulty with the intertemporal theory is the "curse of dimensionality". In going from the static case to the intertemporal case, we have multiplied the dimensionality of our private and government production possibilities sets T^f by a factor of T (approximately). As the number of parameters required to approximate restricted profit and cost functions of the type defined by (46) and (50) to the second order grows as the square of the dimensionality of the goods space, it can readily be seen that it will be virtually impossible to form such second order approximations using econometric techniques.

The results of this section may be summarized as follows: it is relatively easy to extend the static theory of benefit measurement to the intertemporal context, but the practical difficulties in implementing the intertemporal theory are enormous. Thus in empirical work, we will probably be forced to use static techniques, and to cumulate the static benefits using relatively crude discounting techniques. We should keep in mind that this latter technique for measuring the benefits of infrastructure investments will tend to underestimate the true benefits, since our crude procedure will tend to ignore increased output that will occur as firms invest optimally to take advantage of the new infrastructure services.

5.2. The Problem of Endogenous Prices for Local Goods.

Changes in infrastructure services for a regional economy tend to be large discrete changes. Hence infrastructure investment projects will tend to have relatively large effects on the local economy, and hence they may induce systematic changes in the prices of certain goods, which we will call local goods for obvious reasons. Thus holding the price vector p constant as we compare the benefits of different infrastructure investments may not be a good strategy, since some of these prices will change endogenously as the infrastructure vector changes.

We revert to the static model developed in section 2. (The reader is free to reinterpret our static model as a dynamic model as in section 5.1, but we shall deal only with the static model in this section in order to minimize notational complexities). We now interpret the N goods in the $x \equiv (x_1,\ldots,x_N)$ vector as interregionally traded goods which are supplied to (or demanded from) the region in a perfectly elastic manner; i.e., their prices $(p_1,\ldots,p_N) \equiv p$ are fixed. We introduce a second class of M goods into regional economy. Their prices, $(q_1,\ldots,q_M) \equiv q$, depend on local supply and demand conditions. The old firm f restricted profit function defined by (1) is now redefined as:

$$(51) \qquad \pi^f(p,q,s^f,k^f) \equiv \max_{x,y}\{p\cdot x + q\cdot y : (x,y,s^f,k^f) \in T^f\}$$

where $q\cdot y \equiv \Sigma_{m=1}^{M} q_m y_m$, $y \equiv (y_1,\ldots,y_M)$ is a vector of firm net outputs of local goods (if $y_m < 0$, then local good m is being utilized as an input), and all of the other variables are defined as in section 1.

The old government restricted cost function defined by (4) is now redefined as:

$$(52)\quad c(p,q,s^1,\ldots,s^F,k^0) \equiv \min_{x^0,y^0} \{p\cdot x^0 + q\cdot y^0 : (x^0,y^0,s^1,\ldots,s^F,k^0) \in T^0\}$$

where $y^0 \equiv (y_1^0,\ldots,y_M^0) \geq 0_M$ is a vector of government purchases of local goods and q is the vector of local good prices defined above, and all other variables are defined as in section 1.

Now suppose we have an initial allocation of firm infrastructure services vectors for the local economy, $s^{10},s^{20},\ldots,s^{F0}$ where $s^{f0} \equiv (s_1^{f0},s_2^{f0},\ldots s_I^{f0}) \geq 0_I$ represents the allocation received by firm f. Suppose the price vector for internationally traded goods is $p \equiv (p_1,\ldots,p_N) \gg 0$, the government fixed capital stock vector is k^0 and the firm capital stock vectors are $k^1,\ldots,k^F$ and the initial price vector for local goods is $q^0 \equiv (q_1^0,\ldots q_M^0) \gg 0_M$. Suppose x^{f0},y^{f0} solves (51) when $q = q^0$ and $s^f = s^{f0}$ for $f = 1,2,\ldots F$; i.e.,

$$(53)\quad p\cdot x^{f0} + q^0\cdot y^{f0} = \pi^f(p,q^0,s^{f0},k^f),\ f=1,2,\ldots,F.$$

Suppose x^{00},y^{00} solves the government's cost minimization problem (52) when $q = q^0$ and $s^f = s^{f0}$ for $f = 1,\ldots,F$; i.e.,

$$(54)\quad p\cdot x^{00} + q^0\cdot y^{00} = c(p,q^0,s^{10},\ldots,s^{F0},k^0).$$

Finally suppose that the government changes the vectors of firm infrastructure services to $s^{11},s^{21},\ldots,s^{F1}$. How can we measure the potential benefits of the change in infrastructure services, taking into account the endogeneity of the local prices q?

Consider the following constrained maximization problem:

$$(55)\qquad \max_{x^0,x^1,\ldots,x^F,y^0,y^1,\ldots,y^F}\{p\cdot[\Sigma_{f=1}^F x^f - x^0] - p\cdot[\Sigma_{f=1}^F x^{f0} - x^{00}] :$$

$$\Sigma_{f=1}^f y^f - y^0 \geq \Sigma_{f=1}^F y^{f0} - y^{00};\ (x^0,y^0,s^{11},\ldots,s^{F1},k^0) \in T^0;$$

$$(x^f,y^f,s^{f1},k^f) \in T^f \text{ for } f=1,\ldots,F\}$$

$$\equiv B^*(s^{10},\ldots,s^{F0};s^{11},\ldots,s^{1F};p,k^0,k^1,\ldots,k^F)$$

where we have defined the <u>net benefits function</u> B^* of the change in infrastructure services from the s^{f0} allocation to the s^{f1} allocation to be the optimized objective function for problem (55). The objective function in (55) is the increase in the net value of "internationally" traded goods at the constant reference prices p over the initial net value $p\cdot[\Sigma_{f=1}^F x^{f0}-x^{00}]$ that was produced when firm infrastructure services were at the levels $s^{10},\ldots,s^{F0}$. The first set of constraints in (55), $\Sigma_{f=1}^F y^f - y^0 \geq \Sigma_{f=1}^F y^{f0} - y^{00}$, forces the economy with the new levels of firm infrastructure services, $s^{11},s^{21},\ldots,s^{F1}$, to produce <u>at least</u> the preproject level of net outputs for locally traded goods, $\Sigma_{f=1}^F\ y^{f0}-y^{00}$. The remaining constraints in (55) simply force the post project firm net output vectors (x^f,y^f) and the post project government input demand vector (x^0,y^0) to be technologically feasible. (55) defines our new net benefits function which replaces (5). It is a hypothetical construct, because there is no guarantee that the regional economy will choose to produce <u>exactly</u> the old preproject levels of local goods net output, $\Sigma_{f=1}^F y^{f0}-y^{00}$, after the infrastructure project has been undertaken. However, B^* is an interesting pure efficiency measure for the effectiveness of the new infrastructure services allocation. If B^* turned out to be positive, then obviously the new local economy is better off than the old local economy, since the production of domestic outputs has not decreased, the utilization of domestic inputs has not increased (if there are no free goods in the new equilibrium, the aggregate domestic net output will remain unchanged) and the net output of internationally traded goods has increased. Thus the local economy will earn additional foreign exchange, and presumably with an adequate set of tax and transfer instruments, the local government could make everyone better off.

We now attempt to relate our new net benefits measure defined by (55) to our old net benefit measures defined by (5) for various reference prices. The following preliminary result will prove to be useful.

<u>Proposition 5</u>: Suppose the private and public production possibilities sets T^f an T^0 are such that the sets of (x^0,y^0) and (x^f,y^f) which satisfy the constraints in (55) are closed, convex sets. Then the function B* defined by (55) may be written as the optimized objective function for the following minimization problem involving the firm restrited profit functions defined by (51) and the government's restricted cost function defined by (52):

$$(56) \qquad B^*(s^{10},\ldots,s^{F0};s^{11},\ldots,s^{F1};\ p,k^0,k^1,\ldots,k^F) = \min_q\{\Sigma_{f=1}^F \pi^f(p,q,s^{f1},k^f) - c(p,q,s^{11},\ldots,s^{F1},k^0) - p\cdot[\Sigma_{f=1}^F x^{f0}-x^{00}] - q\cdot[\Sigma_{f=1}^F y^{f0}-y^{00}] : q \geq 0_M\}.$$

<u>Corollary 5.1</u>: If the functions π^f and c are differentiable with respect to a, then a solution $q^1 \geq 0_M$ to (56) satisfies the following Kuhn-Tucker [1951] conditions:

(57) $\Sigma_{f=1}^{F}\nabla_q\pi^f(p,q^1,s^{f1},k^f) - \nabla_q c(p,q^1,s^{11},\ldots,s^{F1},k^0) \geq \Sigma_{f=1}^{F}y^{f0}-y^{00}$;

(58) $q^1\cdot\{\Sigma_{f=1}^{F}\nabla_q\pi^f(p,q^1,s^{f1},k^f) - \nabla_q c(p,q^1,s^{11},\ldots,s^{F1},k^0) - \Sigma_{f=1}^{F}y^{f0} + y^{00}\}$
$= 0.$

<u>Corollary 5.2</u>: If the functions π^f and c are differentiable with respect to q at $q^1 \geq 0_M$ and conditions (57) and (58) hold, then q^1 solves the minimization problem (56).

<u>Corollary 5.3</u>: If $q^1 \gg 0_M$, then condition (58) may be dropped from the previous two corollaries and the inequalities in (57) must be changed to equalities.

In view of Hotelling's Lemma (equation (15) in Appendix 1) and Shephard's Lemma (equations (14) in Appendix 2), we see that the equality version of the inequalities in (57) simply represents the first set of constraints in (55); i.e., the post project net supply vector for domestic goods should equal the corresponding pre project vector. The prices q^1 are the equilibrium prices for this set of equations. The more general system of inequalities and equations, (57) and (58), simply makes allowances for the possible existence of free domestic goods.

Inserting a solution $q^1 \geq 0_M$ for (56) into the objective function in (56) yields the following expression for the net benefits of an infrastructure investment project with local goods:

(59) $B^* \equiv \Sigma_{f=1}^{F}\pi^f(p,q^1,s^{f1},k^f) - c(p,q^1,s^{11},\ldots,s^{F1},k^0)$

$$- \Sigma_{f=1}^{F}[p\cdot x^{f0} + q^1\cdot y^{f0}] + [p\cdot x^{00} + q^1\cdot y^{00}].$$

How does B* defined by (55), (56), or (59) compare to the following fixed price benefit measures that are counterparts to (5)?

(60) $$B^0 \equiv \Sigma_{f=1}^{F}\{\pi^f(p,q^0,s^{f1},k^f) - \pi^f(p,q^0,s^{f0},k^f)\}$$
$$- \{c(p,q^0,s^{11},\ldots,s^{F1},k^0) - c(p,q^0,s^{10},\ldots,s^{F0},k^0)\} ;$$

(61) $$B^1 \equiv \Sigma_{f=1}^{F}\{\pi^f(p,q^1,s^{f1},k^f) - \pi^f(p,q^1,s^{f0},k^f)\}$$
$$- \{c(p,q^1,s^{11},\ldots,s^{F1},k^0) - c(p,q^1,s^{10},\ldots,s^{F0},k^0)\}.$$

Note that the net benefit measure (60) uses the preproject prices p, q^0 as constant reference prices while the measure defined by (61) uses the (hypothetical) post project prices p,q^1 as constant reference prices.

Proposition 6: If the technology sets are appropriately convex so that we can apply Proposition 5 and the solution q^1 to (56) is positive (i.e., $q^1 \gg 0_M$), then B* defined by (55), (56) or (59) lies between the two constant price measures defined by (60) and (61); i.e., we have

(62) $$B^1 \leq B^* \leq B^0.$$

Thus using the constant preproject price benefit measure B^0 will tend to overstate the endogenous local price measure B*, while using the constant (hypothetical) post project price measure B^1 will tend to understate the "true" benefits B*. Thus our technique of taking an average of pre and post project benefit measures explained in section 4 above is useful not only for the numerical approximation reasons explained there, but also as a means of more closely approximating the "true" benefit measure B*; i.e., $(1/2)B^0 + (1/2)B^1$ will probably be closer to B* than either B^0 or B^1 taken separately.

We now examine how first and second order approximations to our new endogeneous local price benefit measure defined by (55) compare to first and second order approximations to our old constant price benefit measures of the type defined by (5), two of which are B^0 and B^1 defined by (60) and (61).

<u>Proposition 7</u>: The first order approximations to B* and B^0 around the s^{f0} allocation coincide; i.e., we have

$$(62)\qquad B^*(s^{10},\ldots,s^{F0};s^{11},\ldots,s^{F1};p,k^0,k^1,\ldots,k^F)$$

$$\simeq \Sigma_{f=1}^F\{\nabla_{s^f}\pi^f(p,q^0,s^{f0},k^f) - \nabla_{s^f}c(p,q^0,s^{10},\ldots,s^{F0},k^0)\}\cdot\{s^{f1}-s^{f0}\}$$

$$\equiv \Sigma_{f=1}^F\{w^{f0} - m^{f0}\}\cdot\{s^{f1}-s^{f0}\}$$

$$\simeq B^0.$$

The firm willingness to pay vectors at the preproject allocation are defined by $w^{f0} = \nabla_{s^f}\pi^f(p,q^0,s^{f0},k^f)$, f=1,...,F, and the government's marginal cost vector for supplying firm f is defined by $m^{f0} \equiv \nabla_{s^f}c(p,q^0,s^{10},\ldots,s^{F0},k^0)$

for f=1,...,F. Although the constant price benefit measure B^0 approximates the endogenous price benefit measure B* to the first order, this equality is not maintained when we approximate each measure to the second order around the initial allocation of infrastructure services $s^{10},\ldots,s^{F0}$.

Proposition 8: The second order approximation to the constant price benefit measure B^0 defined by (60) around the initial allocation $s^{10},\ldots,s^{F0}$ is always equal to or greater than the corresponding second order approximation to the endogenous local prices benefit measure B* defined by (56) or (59).

We note that the proof of Proposition 8 in Appendix 4 develops some useful formulae for the second order approximations to B^0 and B*. These formulae may be evaluated if we have a knowledge of the first and second derivatives of the firm profit functions π^f and the government cost function c evaluated at the initial preproject equilibrium.

We may summarize the results of this section as follows. The existence of large infrastructure projects that will affect at least some prices in the regional economy led us to define a new benefit measure B* that recognized the possibility of endogenous prices. However, Proposition 6 shows that our new benefit measure B* will fall nicely between our old constant price benefit measures B^0 and B^1. Proposition 7 told us that to the first order, the new measure is indistinguishable from the old measure B^0, but Proposition 8 told us that to the second order, the old constant price benefit measure will be larger than the new endogenous price benefit measure B*.

We turn now to another major source of difficulty with our original measure of firm benefits (5).

5.3 The Neglect of Consumer Benefits

The construction of a new road or a new water line will benefit not only firms in the project affected area, but also consumers living there. How can we measure the pure efficiency effects of a project when consumers receive benefits from the project?

Our approach to this problem may be explained as follows. We freeze each household at its preproject level of welfare. We then introduce the infrastructure investment project into the regional economy and determine whether additional foreign exchange can now be extracted from the local economy while preserving household utility levels and regional supply equals demand constraints.

We assume that there are H households in the region and that the initial household h infrastructure services consumption vector is $S^{h0} \equiv (S_1^{h0}, S_2^{h0}, \ldots, S_I^{h0}) \geq 0_I$ for $h = 1,\ldots,H$. The government is initially supplying firm f with amounts $s^{f0} \equiv (s_1^{f0}, s_2^{f0}, \ldots, s_I^{f0}) \geq 0_I$ of infrastructure services for $f = 1,2,\ldots,F$. As in the previous section, we assume that the fixed price vector for the N interregionally traded goods is $p \equiv (p_1,\ldots,p_N) \gg 0_N$ and the initial price vector for the M local goods is $q^0 \equiv (q_1^0,\ldots,q_M^0) \gg 0_M$. The old government restricted cost function defined by (52) is now redefined by

$$\text{(63)} \qquad c(p,q,s^1,\ldots,s^F,S^1,\ldots,S^H,k^0) \equiv \min_{x^0,y^0}\{p\cdot x^0 + q\cdot y^0$$

$$= (x^0,y^0,s^1,\ldots,s^F,S^1,\ldots,S^H,k^0) \in T^0\}$$

where k^0 is the government's initial fixed capital stock, and s^f and S^h are the infrastructure service vectors that are to be supplied to firm f and household h respectively. We assume that x^{00},y^{00} solves (63) when we are at the initial period 0 allocation of infrastructure services; i.e.,

$$(64) \qquad p\cdot x^{00} + q^0\cdot y^{00} = c(p,q^0,s^{10},\ldots,s^{F0},S^{10},\ldots,S^{H0},k^0).$$

We assume that consumer preferences over different combinations $c \equiv (c_1, \ldots,c_N)$ of interregionally traded goods, $d \equiv (d_1,\ldots,d_M)$ of locally traded goods and of infrastructure services can be represented by utility functions. Thus if $U^h(c,d,S^h)$ denotes the utility function for household h, we define the corresponding expenditure function m^h by

$$(65) \qquad m^h(u_h,p,q,S^h) \equiv \min_{c,d}\{p\cdot c + q\cdot d : U^h(c,d,S^h) \geq u_h\}$$

for h = 1,2,...,H. For the mathematical properties of expenditure functions, see Appendix 3. We define the initial utility level for household h to be u_h^0 for h = 1,...,H. We also assume that the initial consumption vector (c^{h0},d^{h0}) for household h solves the expenditure minimization problem (65) when $u = u_h^0$, $q = q^0$ and $S^h = S^{h0}$; i.e., we have for h = 1,...,H:

$$(66) \qquad p\cdot c^{h0} + q^0\cdot d^{h0} = m^h\,(u^0,p,q^0,S^{h0}).$$

Finally we assume that x^{f0},y^{f0} solves the firm f restricted profit maximization problem (51) when $q = q^0$ and $s^f = s^{f0}$, so that relations (53) continue to hold.

We wish to define a net benefit measure B for a change in the government's supply of infrastructure services to firms and households from the initial allocation $s^{10},\ldots,s^{F0},S^{10},\ldots,S^{H0}$ to a new allocation $s^{11},\ldots,$ $s^{F1},S^{11},\ldots,S^{H1}$. Consider the following constrained maximization problem (67) (which is the extension of (55) to cover the case of consumer benefits):

$$(67)\quad \max_{x^0,x^1,\ldots,x^F,y^0,y^1,\ldots y^F,c^1,\ldots,c^H,d^1,\ldots,d^H}\{p\cdot[\Sigma_{f=1}^F x^f - x^0 - \Sigma_{h=1}^H c^h] - p\cdot[\Sigma_{f=1}^F x^{f0} - x^{00} - \Sigma_{h=1}^H c^{h0}] : \Sigma_{f=1}^F y^f - y^0 - \Sigma_{h=1}^H d^h - \bar{y} \geq 0_M;\ (x^0,y^0,s^{11},\ldots,s^{F1},S^{11},\ldots,S^{H1},k^0)\ \varepsilon\ T^0;$$

$$(x^f,y^f,s^{f1},k^f)\ \varepsilon\ T^f \text{ for } f=1,\ldots,F;\ U^h(c^h,d^h,S^{h1}) \geq u_h^0 \text{ for } h = 1,2,\ldots,H\}$$

$$\equiv B^*(s^{10},\ldots,s^{F0},s^{11},\ldots,s^{F1},S^{10},\ldots,S^{H0},S^{11},\ldots,S^{H1},p,\bar{y},u_1^0,\ldots,u_H^0),$$

where we have defined our new <u>net benefits function</u> B^* to be the optimized value of the objective function for (67). B^* also depends on the fixed capital stock vectors $k^0,k^1,\ldots,k^F$, but since these are being held constant, we need not mention them explicitly. The objective function in (67) is the net supply of internationally traded goods less household and government demands, $p\cdot[\Sigma_{f=1}^F x^f - x^0 - \Sigma_{h=1}^H c^h]$ minus the economy's initial net supply of internationally traded goods less government and household demands, $p\cdot[\Sigma_{f=1}^F x^{f0} - x^{00} - \Sigma_{h=1}^H c^{h0}]$. The first set of constraints in (67) represents the supply equal to or greater than demand constraints for the local goods in the economy (the vector $\bar{y} \equiv (\bar{y}_1,\ldots,\bar{y}_M)$ represents an <u>endowment</u> vector of local goods for the regional economy); the next set of constraints represents the government technology constraints given that the government will now supply services $s^{11},\ldots,s^{F1}$ to firms and services $S^{11},\ldots,S^{H1}$ to households; the next set of constraints represents the firm technological constraints; and the final set of constraints ensures that each household will attain its preproject level of welfare, u_h^0 for household h. If B* turns out to be positive, then the project (i.e., the change in infrastructure services from $s^{10},\ldots,s^{F0},S^{10},\ldots,S^{H0}$ to $s^{11},\ldots,s^{F1},S^{11},\ldots,S^{H1}$) is obviously <u>potentially beneficial</u> since the economy's resource constraints are respected, each household has at least its old welfare level. and the government ends up with extra foreign exchange, which presumably can be used to increase welfare. However, it is important to remember that the solution to (67) gives a hypothetical allocation of resources that need not be realized in period 1.

We shall assume that the endowment vector $\bar{y}$ in (67) satisfies the following equaton:

$$(68)\qquad \bar{y} = \Sigma_{f=1}^{F} y^{f0} - y^{00} - \Sigma_{h=1}^{H} d^{h0}.$$

Thus we are implicitly assuming that the economy's period 0 endowment vector of domestic goods is also applicable to the economy represented in the constrained maximization problem (67).

The following Proposition is a counterpart to Proposition 5.

<u>Proposition 9</u>: Suppose $\bar{y}$ is defined by (68) and B* is defined by (67). Suppose also that $T^0,T^1,\ldots T^F$ and $U^1,\ldots,U^H$ are such that the feasible $(x^0,y^0),(x^f,y^f)$ and (c^h,d^h) sets defined by the last three sets of constraints

in (67) are closed convex sets (closedness and convexity of the sets $T^0, T^1, \ldots, T^F$ and continuity and quasiconcavity of the utility functions U^h will ensure this). Finally assume that a feasible solution for (67) exists which satisfies the M inequality constraints in (67) strictly. Then B* may be expressed as the optimized objective function for the following minimization problem involving the firm profit functions π^f defined by (51), the government's cost function c defined by (63) and the consumer expenditure functions m^h defined by (65):

$$(69) \quad B^* = \min_{q \geq 0_M} \{\Sigma_{f=1}^F \pi^f(p,q,s^{f1},k^f) - c(p,q,s^{11},\ldots,s^{F1},S^{11},\ldots,S^{H1},k^0)$$
$$-\Sigma_{h=1}^H m^h(u_h^0,p,q,S^{h1}) - p\cdot[\Sigma_{f=1}^F x^{f0}-x^{00}] + p\cdot[\Sigma_{h=1}^H c^{h0}]$$
$$-q\cdot[\Sigma_{f=1}^F y^{f0}-y^{00}] + q\cdot[\Sigma_{h=1}^H d^{h0}]\}.$$

<u>Corollary 9.1</u>: If the functions π^f, c, and m^h are differentiable with respect to the components of q, then a positive solution $q^1 \gg 0_M$ to the minimization problem (69) satisfies the following first order necessary conditions:

$$(70) \quad \Sigma_{f=1}^F \nabla_q \pi^f(p,q^1,s^{f1},k^f) - \nabla_q c(p,q^1,s^{11},\ldots,s^{F1},S^{11},\ldots,S^{H1},k^0)$$
$$-\Sigma_{h=1}^H \nabla_q m^h(u_h^0,p,q^1,S^{h1}) = \Sigma_{f=1}^F y^{f0}-y^{00}-\Sigma_{h=1}^H d^{h0}.$$

Using (15) in Appendix 1, we know that the vector of derivatives $\nabla_q \pi^f$ which appears in (70) is producer f's vector of profit maximizing net supply functions for domestic goods. Using (15) in Appendix 2, we see that the vector of derivatives $\nabla_q c$ is the government's vector of cost minimizing demands for domestic goods. Using property (2) in Appendix 3, we see that the vector of derivatives $\nabla_q m^h$ which appears in (70) is household h's vector of expenditure minimizing net demand functions (or Hicksian net demand functions) for domestic goods, conditional on household h receiving the vector S^{h1} of infrastructure services. Thus the system of equations (70) is the system of M net supply equals demand equations for domestic goods which determines the equilibrium domestic price vector $q^1 \equiv (q_1^1, q_2^1, \ldots, q_M^1)$ for the regional economy's hypothetic equilibrium associated with the new infrastructure services allocation represented by the I dimensional vectors $s^{11}, \ldots, s^{F1}, S^{11}, \ldots, S^{H1}$.

Inserting a solution q^1 to the minimization problem (69) yields the following expression for the net benefits of a change in the allocation of infrastructure services from the initial allocation $s^{10}, \ldots, s^{F0}, S^{10}, \ldots S^{H0}$ to the new allocation $s^{11}, \ldots, s^{F1}, S^{11}, \ldots, S^{H1}$:

$$(71) \qquad B^* = \Sigma_{f=1}^F \{\pi^f(p, q^1, s^{f1}, k^f\} - p \cdot x^{f0} - q^1 \cdot y^{f0}\}$$

$$- \{c(p, q^1, s^{11}, \ldots s^{F1}, S^{11}, \ldots, S^{H1}, k^0) - p \cdot x^{00} - q^1 \cdot y^{00}\}$$

$$- \Sigma_{h=1}^H \{m^h(u_h^0, p, q^1, S^{h1}) - p \cdot c^{h0} - q^1 \cdot d^{h0}\}.$$

Formula (71) is valid for large changes in the allocation of infrastructure services and no differentiability restrictions are required for its validity. However, we do require the relatively weak restrictions listed in Proposition 9 above.

How does the endogenous price measure of benefits defined by (69) or (71) compare to the following fixed price benefit measures that are the natural extensions to the entire economy of our old firm constant price benefit measures defined by (5)?

(72) $$B^0 \equiv \Sigma_{f=1}^F\{\pi^f(p,q^0,s^{f1},k^f) - \pi^f(p,q^0,s^{f0},k^f)\}$$
$$-\{c(p,q^0,s^{11},\ldots,s^{F1},S^{11},\ldots,S^{H1},k^0) - c(p,q^0,s^{10},\ldots s^{F0},S^{10},\ldots,S^{H0},k^0)\}$$
$$- \Sigma_{h=1}^H\{m^h(u_h^0,p,q^0,S^{h1}) - m^h(u_h^0,p,q^0,S^{h0})\};$$

(73) $$B^1 \equiv \Sigma_{f=1}^F\{\pi^f(p,q^1,s^{f1},k^f) - \pi^f(\pi,q^1,s^{f0},k^f)\}$$
$$-\{c(p,q^1,s^{11},\ldots,s^{F1},S^{11},\ldots,S^{H1},k^0) - c(p,q^1,s^{10},\ldots s^{F0},S^{10},\ldots,S^{H0},k^0)\}$$
$$- \Sigma_{h=1}^H\{m^h(u_h^0,p,q^1,S^{h1})-m^h(u^0,p,q^1,S^{h0})\} .$$

Note that the constant reference prices in (72) are the pre project prices p,q^0 while the reference prices in (73) are the post project prices p,q^1 where q^1 is a solution to (69) and thus is the price vector for local goods in the post project hypothetical economy that is associated with the post project allocation of infrastructure services $s^{11},\ldots,s^{F1},S^{11},\ldots,S^{H1}$ and the pre project distribution of real income $u_1^0,\ldots,u_H^0$.

Proposition 10: Suppose the hypotheses of Proposition 9 hold and in addition, the solution q^1 to (69) is positive; i.e., $q^1 \gg 0_M$. Then B* defined by (69) or (71) lies between the two constant price benefit measures defined by (72) and (73); i.e., we have

(74) $$B^1 \leq B^* \leq B^0.$$

The above Proposition is valid for large projects and does not require any differentiability assumptions. As was the case with Proposition 6, $(1/2)B^0 + (1/2)B^1$ will probably be closer to the "true" benefit measure B* than either B^0 to B^1 taken separately.

We now examine how first and second order approximations to our new endogenous local price benefit measure B* defined by (67) or (69) compare to first and second order approximations of the constant price benefit measure B^0 defined by (72).

Proposition 11: The first order approximations to B* and B^0 around the preproject allocation of infrastructure services coincide; i.e., we have

$$B^*(s^{11},\ldots,s^{F1},S^{11},\ldots,S^{H1})$$

$$\simeq \Sigma_{f=1}^{F}\{\nabla_{s^f}\pi^f(p,q^0,s^{f0},k^0) - \nabla_{s^f}c(p,q^0,s^{10},\ldots,s^{F0},S^{10},\ldots,S^{H0},k^0)\}\cdot\{s^{f1}-s^{f0}\}$$

$$+ \Sigma_{h=1}^{H}\{-\nabla_{S^h}m^h(u_h^0,p,q^0,S^{h0}) - \nabla_{S^h}c(p,q^0,s^{10},\ldots,s^{F0},S^{10},\ldots S^{H0},k^0)\}\cdot\{S^{h1} - S^{h0}\}$$

$$(75) \quad \equiv \Sigma_{f=1}^{F}\{w^{f0} - m^{f0}\}\cdot\{s^{f1}-s^{f0}\} + \Sigma_{h=1}^{H}\{W^{h0}-M^{h0}\}\cdot\{S^{h1}-S^{h0}\}$$

$$\simeq B^0(s^{11},\ldots,s^{F1},S^{11},\ldots,S^{H1}).$$

In definition (67), B* is a function of many variables, including $s^{11},\ldots,s^{F1}$ and $S^{11},\ldots,S^{H1}$. In (75), these other variables are held constant, so we have suppressed mention of them. Similarly, in definition (72), B^0 is a function of many variables in addition to the s^{f1} and S^{h1}. In (75), these other variables are held constant. In (75), we have defined producer f's initial <u>willingness to pay</u> for infrastructure services vector as $w^{f0} \equiv \nabla_{s^f}\pi^f(p,q^0\ s^{f0},k^f)$; see equation (31) in Appendix 1, where we also indicated that w^{f0} would be nonnegative if the firm f production possibilities set T^f satisfied a free disposal assumption. In (75), we also defined the government's firm f marginal cost vector by $m^{f0} = \nabla_{s^f} c(p,q^0,s^{10},\ldots,s^{F0},S^{10}$ $S^{H0},\ k^0)$ and the marginal cost vector for producing infrastructure services for household h by $M^{h0} \equiv \nabla_{S^h}c(p,q_s^0,s^{10},\ldots,s^{F0},S^{10},\ldots,S^{H0},k^0)$; see equation (20) in appendix 2, where we also indicated that m^{f0} an M^{h0} would be non-negative vectors if the government production possibilities set T^0 satisfied a free disposal property. Finally, in (75) we have defined household h's initial <u>willingness to pay</u> for infrastructure services vector as $W^{h0} \equiv -\nabla_{S^h}m^h(u_h^0,p,q^0,S^{h0})$; see equation (6) in Appendix 3. Proposition 3 in Appendix 3 indicated that W^{h0} would be nonnegative if the household h utility function U^h satisfied a certain free disposal property.

Note that the first order approximation to B* or B^0 defined by (75) can readily be formed provided that we know: (i) the initial allocation of infrastructure services across firms and households, $s^{10},\ldots,s^{F0}$ and $S^{10},\ldots,$ S^{H0}, (ii) the post project allocation of infrastructure services across firms and households, $s^{11},\ldots,s^{F1}$ and $S^{11},\ldots,S^{H1}$, (iii) the initial producer willingness to pay vectors w^{h0}, (iv) the initial consumer willingness to pay vectors W^{h0}, and (v) the initial marginal cost of producing extra units of infrastructure services vectors for firms m^{f0} and for households M^{h0}.

Although the constant price benefit measure B^0 approximates the endogenous price benefit measure B* to the first order, this equality is not maintained when we approximate each measure to the second order around the initial allocation of infrastructure services, as is shown in the following Proposition.

Proposition 12: The second order approximation to the constant price benefit measure B^0 defined by (72) around the initial infrastructure services allocation $s^{10},\ldots,s^{F0},S^{10},\ldots,S^{H0}$ is always equal to or greater than the corresponding second order approximation to the endogenous local prices benefit measure B* defined by (69).

We provide explicit expressions for the second order approximations to B^0 and B* in Appendix 4. These formulae may be evaluated if we have a knowledge of the first and second derivatives of the firm profit functions π^f, the government's cost function c, and the household expenditure functions m^h evaluated at the initial preproject equilibrium.

The second order approximation to B* (call it $\tilde{B}^*$) is particularly useful, since it may be used to guide government investment in infrastructure policies, e.g., consider the following constrained maximization problem involving the second order approximation to B*:

$$\text{(76)}\qquad \max_{s^{11},\ldots,s^{F1},S^{11},\ldots,S^{H1}} \{\tilde{B}^*(s^{11},\ldots,s^{F1},S^{11},\ldots,S^{H1}):\ s^{f1} \geq 0_I \text{ for } f=1,\ldots,F;\ S^{h1} \geq 0_I \text{ for } h = 1,\ldots,H\}.$$

The constrained maximization problem (76) is a quadratic programming problem (see Dantzig [1963;490-497] for discussion and an algorithm). Moreover, if the firm technology sets T^f and the government technology set T^0 are convex and the household utility functions U^h are quasiconcave (see (7) in Appendix 3 for a definition of quasiconcavity), then it can be shown that (76) is a concave quadratic programming problem, and the Dantzig algorithm will solve (76) rather easily. The resulting solution to (76) would provide the government with an <u>approximately optimal infrastructure investment policy.</u>

Recall that the first order approximation to $B^*(s^{11},\ldots,s^{F1},S^{11},\ldots,S^{H1})$ was defined by (75). This formula may be used to derive necessary conditions for the optimality of the initial infrastructure services allocation $s^{10},\ldots,$ $,\ldots,s^{F0},S^{10},\ldots,S^{H0}$. Thus if B^* is at a maximum with respect to $s^{11},\ldots,s^{1F}$ $S^{11},\ldots,S^{H1}$ at the initial allocation, and the initial allocation is positive so that $s^{f0} \gg 0_I$ for $f = 1,\ldots,F$ and $S^{h0} \gg 0_I$ for $h = 1,\ldots,H$, then the following <u>optimality conditions</u> will be satisfied:

$$(77) \qquad \nabla_{s^{f1}} B^*(s^{10},\ldots,s^{F0},S^{10},\ldots,S^{H0}) = w^{f0} - m^{f0} = 0_I,\ f = 1,\ldots,F;$$

$$(78) \qquad \nabla_{S^{h1}} B^*(s^{10},\ldots,s^{F0},S^{10},\ldots,S^{H0}) = W^{h0} - M^{H0} = 0_I,\ h = 1,\ldots,H,$$

where the vectors w^{f0},m^{f0},M^{h0} and W^{h0} were defined below (75). If $q^0 \gg 0_M$, then (70) will also hold except that q^1,S^{h1} and the s^{f1} are replaced by q^0, S^{h0} and the s^{f0}.

If $s_i^{f0} = 0$, then the ith equation in (77) for this index f is replaced by Kuhn-Tucker optimality condition, $w_i^{f0} - m_i^{f0} \leq 0$. If $S_i^{h0} = 0$, then the ith equation in (78) for this index h is replaced by the optimality condition $W_i^{h0} - M_i^{h0} \leq 0$.

If all firms are able to consume the same vector of infrastructure services so that $s^f = s$ for all f, then the F conditions (77) collapse down to the following condition:

$$(79) \qquad \nabla_s B^*(s^0, S^{10}, \ldots, S^{H0}) = \Sigma_{f=1}^F w^{f0} - m^0 = 0_I$$

where $m^0 \equiv m^{f0}$ is the common vector of marginal costs and $s^0 \equiv s^{f0} \gg 0_I$ is the common vector of firm infrastructure services. Conditions (79) correspond to optimality conditions derived by Kaizuka [1965] and Sandmo [1972].

If all households are able to consume the same vector of infrastructure services so that $S^h = S$ for all h, then the H optimality conditions (78) collapse down to the following condition:

$$(80) \qquad \nabla_S B^*(s^{10}, \ldots, s^{F0}, S^0) = \Sigma_{h=1}^H W^{h0} - M^0 = 0_I$$

where $M^0 \equiv M^{h0}$ is the common vector of marginal cost and $S^0 \equiv S^{h0} \gg 0_I$ is the common vector of household infrastructure services. The I equations in (80) correspond to Samuelson's [1964] conditions for the <u>optimal provision of public goods to consumers</u>. Hence we may interpret conditions (79) as the corresponding conditions for the optimal provision of public goods to producers in the case where all producers are able to consume the common producer vector of infrastructure services.

If all consumers and all producers are able to consume exactly the same vector of infrastructure services so that $s^f = s = S = S^h$ for all f and h, then the F plus H optimality conditions (77) and (78) collapse to the following single optimality condition:

$$(81) \qquad \Sigma_{f=1}^{F} w^{f0} + \Sigma_{h=1}^{H} W^{h0} = m^0 = M^0$$

where $m^0 = M^0 \equiv \nabla_s c(p,q^0,s^0,k^0)$ is the common vector of marginal costs and $s^0 = s^{f0} = S^{h0} \gg 0_I$ is the common vector of infrastructure services that is initially supplied to all firms and households in the regional economy.

Thus our general model contains the usual public good models as special cases.

Finally, we note that our open economy model can readily be specialized to the case of a closed economy: we need only let N = 1 and set $p = p_1 = 1$, so that our single internationally traded good may now be interpreted as a numeraire domestic good.

Notes.

One of the best references on intertemporal producer theory is still Hicks [1946;325-328]. The general intertemporal producer model that we suggested in section 5.1 follows that of Hicks. More theoretically restrictive, but more empirically tractable, models may be found in Dorfman, Samuelson and Solow [1958;ch.12], Diewert and Lewis [1982] and Diewert [1985b].

Our user cost of capital formula (49) is similar to the discrete time formula derived in Diewert [1980;471]. For continuous time user cost of capital formulae, see Jorgenson [1963], Smith [1963] and Mohr [1985]. These four references also deal with the complications which result when firms face business income taxes. See also section 8.5 below.

Our approach to the evaluation of infrastructure investment projects outlined in section 5.2 is similar to Diewert's [1983a] <u>productive efficiency</u> approach to project evaluation. The case where each firm is able to consume the same vector of infrastructure services, so that $s^f = s$ for $f = 1,\ldots,F$, is the pure public goods in production case. This pure public goods case was considered in the context of a distorted economy by Tsuneki [1984].

Tsuneki [1984] also considered the pure public goods case with consumers also sharing the common service vector s that we considered in section 5.3. The general approach pursued in section 5.3 is an adaptation of the approaches of Allais [1943][1977] and Debreu [1951][1954] to the measurement of the benefits of removing distortions from an economy. The approaçhes of Allais and Debreu were unified by Diewert [1981a][1984c] and Auerbach [1982]. The Allais-Debreu approach to project evaluation developed in section 5.3 may be found in Kanemoto and Mera [1984], Kanemoto [1985] and Diewert [1984b] in addition to Tsuneki [1984]. Diewert [1984b] calls the Allais-Debreu approach the efficiency approach to project evaluation, and he relates it to the potential Pareto improvement criteria developed by Bruce and Harris [1982] and Diewert [1983a].

The approximately optimal infrastructure investment policy generated by solving the quadratic program (76) is a generalization of Diewert's [1984b] approximately optimal project scale.

Econometric techniques for estimating consumer's preference functions with infrastructure services or public goods as arguments are outlined in Diewert [1978;31-33] and Kanemoto [1985].

An important limitation of our analysis is the absence of tax and monopolistic distortions. Tsuneki [1984] deals with these complications in the context of his public goods investment model as does Diewert [1984b] in the context of his simple project evaluation model.

6. Alternative Approaches to Benefit Measurement

In this section, we list some of the alternative empirical approaches that could be used to measure the benefits of infrastructure investments. We also list some of the difficulties associated with each approach. The reason for putting this section so late in the paper is that before we measure something, we first must have a precise theoretical concept for what we are trying to measure. Thus in this section, we shall draw heavily on the theoretical benefit measures defined in the earlier sections of this paper.

6.1 The Questionnaire or Sample Survey Approach

The three main theoretical benefit measures that we have considered in this paper were (5), (55) and (67). The simplest benefit measure (5) requires information only on the firm restricted profit functions π^f and the government's cost function c. The endogenous price firm benefit measure (55) also requires information on the regional economy's initial net production vectors of local goods. The general equilibrium benefit measure defined by

(67) requires additional information on household expenditure functions m^h, which provide an alternative representation of household utility functions U^h.

We saw in section 3 that a knowledge of firm willingness to pay functions was essentially equivalent to a knowledge of the firm restricted profit functions. In a similar manner, we could show that a knowledge of the government's marginal cost functions is sufficient to determine the restricted cost function, and a knowledge of the household willingness to pay functions is sufficient to determine household expenditure functions up to an additive constant. Thus our first approach to measuring the benefits of infrastructure investments is to simply <u>ask</u> firms and households what their willingness to pay functions are and to ask government production managers what their marginal cost functions are.

This straightforward questionnaire approach suffers from a number of difficulties.

The first difficulty is the incentive compatibility problem mentioned in section 1; i.e., it may be difficult to get producers and consumers to reveal their true willingness to pay functions, since it may well be in their best interests to behave strategically. Theoretically, this problem of strategic behaviour can be eliminated if the rather complex questionnaire technique based on the Groves [1976] mechanism due to Green, Kohlberg and Laffont [1975] and explained in Varian [1978;203] is used. However, the scheme is so complex, that it may be difficult to explain it to producers and consumers. There are also theoretical difficulties with this technique in the intertemporal context, when we do not know exactly what will happen in the future.

A second difficulty is that we want entire willingness to pay schedules, as functions of various exogenous variables. It may be difficult to explain to producers and consumers the conditional nature of the desired willingness to pay functions. Moreover, it may be very costly or virtually impossible for producers to undertake the necessary internal computations to calculate their willingness to pay for an extra unit of infrastructure services, conditional on hypothetically possessing various quantities of other infrastructure services.

A final difficulty with the questionnaire approach is that the potential users of a new infrastructure service that may be supplied to a region may not be present in the survey area when the questionnaire is distributed. This difficulty also applies to the approaches outlined below in sections 6.4, 6.5 and 6.6.

6.2 Ex Post Accounting Approaches

In section 4, we identified a number of _direct_ ex post accounting approaches for measuring the benefits to a firm of an infrastructure investment; e.g., see the first order approximation formulae (29) and (30) and the second order approximation formula (39). These formulae depend on information about the utilization of infrastructure services by firms during the two periods being compared and the corresponding willingness to pay vectors. An extension of the firm approximate gross benefits measure (29) to an approximate aggregate firm net benefits measure is provided by formula (62). An extension of the net benefits measure to include consumers is provided by (75).

In section 4, we also derived a number of _indirect_ ex post accounting formulae for measuring the benefits to a firm of an infrastructure services change; e.g., see the first order approximation formulae (34) and (35) and the second order approximation formula (45). These indirect approaches require information on the firm's production of outputs and utilization of variable inputs during the two periods as well as information on the corresponding prices. We did not pursue these indirect ex post accounting approaches to approximate the general equilibrium benefit measure (67), but this could be done.

The primary advantage to these accounting approaches to benefit measurement is their simplicity: they require only potentially observable price and quantity data for the two situations that are being compared.

Of course, there are a number of disadvantages as well. The first is that the second order approaches are limited to the ex post evaluation of projects, and hence they are useless for planning purposes; i.e., for guiding infrastructure investment in an optimal way. (The first order formulae (29), (34), (62) and (75) do not suffer from this defect, but they have the drawback of being only first order approximations).

A second major difficulty is that the consumer and producer willingness to pay vectors at the initial allocation, W^{h0} and w^{f0}, may be impossible to observe, particularly for categories of infrastructure services that are not being supplied in period 0. Hence we will be forced to make guesses for these vectors, and as a result, the validity of our approximate benefit measures will be severely impaired.

A third difficulty is that the dynamic version of these approximate benefit measures will be virtually impossible to evaluate, since we cannot observe future planned quantities in the current period.

6.3 Engineering and Mathematical Programming Approaches

In this approach, the firm production possibilities sets T^f in (1) and the government's production possibilities set T^0 in (4) are described by convex combinations of discrete vectors or activities. These activity vectors are constructed on the basis of best practice engineering information. For references to the engineering approach to production function or technology set modelling, see Berndt and Wood [1979] and Hoffman and Jorgenson [1977]. The firm variable profit functions π^f defined by (1) and the government's restricted cost function c defined by (4) are defined as solutions to these mathematical programming problems, where the sets T^f and T^0 are described in terms of engineering data. The net firm benefits function B defined by (5) can be defined in terms of the "engineering data" determined functions π^f and c (or more directly in terms of the sets T^f and T^0). The endogenous price firm net benefits function B* can also be defined directly in terms of the sets T^f and T^0 as the solution to a mathematical programming problem.

Although the engineering approach to benefit measurement is easy to describe, it is not easy to implement. It may be very difficult to form accurate estimates of the relevant technology sets using engineering information. In every regional economy there are thousands of goods and thousands of alternative processes to be evaluated. The pure engineering approach does not allow one to use prices to aggregate goods into a smaller, more manageable number of goods. (However, for an "impure" engineering approach, see Kopp and Smith [1983].) Thus the engineering approach may well lead one into an overwhelming amount of detail and complexity. In order to reduce the complexity, our engineers implementing this approach to benefit measurement will have to take various dubious shortcuts and make subjective judgements. Thus the final benefit measures which emerge may be unreliable.

A second major difficulty is that the approach ignores consumer benefits. However, this defect could be overcome by marrying the engineering approach on the technology side to the econometric or revealed preference approaches on the consumer side; e.g., see Manne [1977] and Ginsburgh and Waelbroeck [1981].

6.4 The Applied General Equilibrium Modelling Approach

In the applied general equilibrium modelling approach to the evaluation of alternative government policies such as alternative investment in infrastructure strategies, functional forms are assumed for producer production functions (or their dual profit functions), for government production functions (or their dual cost functions) and for household utility functions (or their dual expenditure functions). The parameters which describe these functional forms are chosen so that the general equilibrium model replicates exactly the data for a base situation. The chosen functional forms are usually of the Cobb-Douglas, Leontief (or fixed coefficients), or C.E.S. (constant elasticity of substitution) type. For the Cobb-Douglas and Leontief functional forms, the base period data suffice to determine all unknown parameters. For the C.E.S. functional form, the base period data must be augmented by estimates (based on econometric investigations) for various elasticities of substitution. The calibration procedures are well explained in Mansur and Whalley [1984]. The entire approach is well surveyed by Shoven and Whalley [1984].

Obviously this calibration procedure could be applied to our firm benefit measures (5) and (55) and to our more general benefit measure defined by (67). The resulting programming problems would be easier to solve than the full blown general equilibrium models that appear in the applied G.E. modelling literature, since we do not require the existence of equilibrium prices in our measures (55) and (67), and hence the burdensome computation of fixed points is avoided.

Jorgenson [1984a] and Lau [1984a] both directed some criticisms against the calibration approach, criticisms that are equally valid in our present context. They observed that the assumed functional forms are too restrictive and are frequently rejected by econometric tests that use less restrictive functional forms. In principle, flexible functional forms (i.e., ones that can provide a second order approximation) could be used in the calibration approach rather than the Cobb-Douglas or Leontief functional forms, but then we are faced with the problem of estimating the parameters which determine the substitution matrices (such as $\nabla^2_{pp}\pi^f(p,s^f,k^f)$, $\nabla^2_{pp}c(p,s^1,\ldots,s^F,k^0)$ etc.) for these flexible functional forms. Thus when we try to introduce flexible functional forms into the calibration approach, we are led directly into the econometric approach.

Another difficulty with the calibration approach to infrastructure benefit measurement is the following one (which is a difficulty with many of the other approaches as well). The problem is that the producer (and consumer) willingness to pay vectors may not be observable in the base period, particularly for infrastructure services that are supplied at zero levels in the base period. The calibration method for the most part requires complete price and quantity data for the base period. Although we can observe the zero quantity components for unsupplied infrastructure services, we cannot readily observe the corresponding prices.

6.5 The Differential Approach

Hicks [1946;313-319] and Harberger [1974] developed an alternative to the applied general equilibrium calibration approach to modelling. This alternative approach also assumes that we have collected the data which characterize an initial equilibrium for our model. However, instead of using fixed point algorithms to calculate alternative hypothetical equilibria, the supply equals demand equations in the model are linearized around the initial equilibrium using the differential calculus. The resulting linearized model provides a first order approximation to the changes in equilibrium prices and quantities induced by changes in exogenous variables and a second order approximation to the induced changes in profits, costs and welfares. It seems appropriate to call this approach to general equilibrium modelling, the *differential approach*.

A differential approach to modelling the effects of changes in infrastructure can be extracted from sections 5.2 and 5.3 above. A second order approximation to the endogenous price firm benefit measure defined by (55) was derived in Proposition 8. Similarly, a second order approximation to the general benefit measure defined by (67) was derived in Proposition 12. Explicit formulae for these second order approximations may be found in Appendix 4.

The primary advantage of the differential approach over the approach explained in section 6.4 is that the differential approach is much easier to implement computationally: all that is required is a matrix inversion whereas the applied general equilibrium modelling approach usually requires the computation of a fixed point or in our case, it requires that a nonlinear programming problem be solved.

However, the differential approach to modelling suffers from the same defect as the applied G.E. modelling approch: we require information on various elasticities of supply and demand evaluated at the initial equilibrium; i.e., we require information on the parameters which characterize the matrices of second order partial derivatives of the profit, cost and expenditure functions in our model. This information is very difficult to obtain.

An advantage of the differential approach to modelling over the computable general equilibrium modelling approach described in section 6.4 is that it is much easier to undertake a sensitivity analysis in the former approach; see Diewert [1985c;section 5]. In a sensitivity analysis, we can vary some or all of the parameters which characterize the second order derivatives in our model and then recompute the equilibrium or in our case, recompute the benefit measure. In the differential approach to sensitivity analysis, we can actually compute the first order partial derivatives of the second order order approximation to our underlying benefit function with respect to the first and second order parameters in our model.

Of course a major disadvantage of the differential approach is that it may not be very accurate for large changes in the policy variables under consideration.

6.6 The Econometric Approach

In this approach to benefit measurement, we collect time series or cross section data, assume functional forms for the firm restricted profit functions π^f, for the government's restricted cost function c and for the household expenditure functions m^h (or for the corresponding dual indirect utility functions), and then we econometrically estimate the unknown parameters which characterize these functional forms. We should attempt to choose functional forms that are flexible; i.e., they can provide a second order approximation to an arbitrary twice continuously differentiable function with the appropriate theoretical homogeneity and curvature properties. Examples of appropriate functional forms may be found in Diewert [1969] [1974] [1978] [1982] and Diewert and Wales [1984]. An empirical example of a general equilibrium model that uses flexible functional forms may be found in Jorgenson [1984a].

If the researcher does not use flexible functional forms, then unwarranted a priori restrictions on elasticities of substitution will be imposed. For example, the use of the Cobb-Douglas, Leontief or C.E.S. functional forms does not allow any pair of goods to be complements; see Hicks [1946;311-312] for a technical definition of complementarity). This is restrictive, since in empirical work using flexible funcional forms involving more than three goods, we generally find that at least one pair of goods are complements.

We have seen earlier in this section that the econometric approach seems to offer our best chance for determining the second order parameters which characterize substitution possibilities in production and consumption. Thus we shall pursue this approach in more detail in the remainder of this paper.

However, we shall restrict ourselves to the case where we wish to estimate a firm restricted profit function π^f. The issues and techniques involved in estimating the government's restricted cost function c are very similar to the profit function case; in fact, we may define $\pi = -c$ and estimate minus the cost function which will have the same properties as a restricted profit function. More explicitly, replace the nonnegative input vector x which appears in Appendix 2 by -x, change the minimization problem to a maximization problem, and c will become a restricted profit function (equal to the negative of cost). We will not deal with the problems involved in estimating household preferences. The reader is referred to Diewert [1978;31-32] for some household modelling techniques that are applicable in the present context.

A major difficulty with the econometric approach is that it requires lots of data. Additional difficulties will be discussed in later sections.

7. The Selection of a Functional Form in the Econometric Approach

7.1 General Issues

In this section, we want to find methods for determining the firm technology set T^f or the dual restricted profit function $\pi^f(p,s^f,k^f) \equiv \max_x \{p\cdot x : (x,s^f,k^f)\in T^f\}$ where $x \equiv (x_1,\ldots,x_N)$ respresents a vector of variable outputs and inputs (if $x_i < 0$, good i is an input), $s^f \geq 0_I$ represents a nonnegative vector of infrastructure services utilization by the firm and $k^f \geq 0_J$ represents a nonnegative vector of fixed capital stocks. The vector $p \equiv (p_1,\ldots,p_N) \gg 0_N$ is the positive vector of variable goods prices that the firm faces. To simplify the notation, we drop the firm superscript f in what follows.

The firm technology set may be represented by means of a production function g, i.e.,

$$(82) \qquad x_1 = g(x_2,x_3,\ldots,x_N,s_1,\ldots,s_I,k_1,\ldots,k_J)$$

where x_1 represents the maximum amount of output 1 that can be produced (or minus the minimal amount of input 1 that is required if $x_1 < 0$) given that the firm has to produce (or utilize if $x_n < 0$) amounts x_n of the other variable goods for $n = 2,3,\ldots,N$ and has available the infrastructure services $(s_1,\ldots,s_I) \equiv s$ and the "fixed" stocks $(k_1,\ldots,k_J) \equiv k$.

The reader may well ask: why do we not simply assume a functional form for g, collect a time series of data for say T periods for $x^t \equiv (x_1^t,x_2^t,\ldots,x_N^t)$, $s^t \equiv (s_1^t,\ldots,s_I^t)$ and $k^t \equiv (k_1^t,\ldots,k_J^t)$, $t = 1,2,\ldots T$, add a stochastic term e^t to the right hand side of (82) when evaluated using the period t data, and then econometrically estimate the unknown parameters for the production function g?

We do not recommend the above procedure for two reasons. The first reason has to do with the problem of degrees of freedom. In order for our functional form for g to be able to provide a second order approximation to an arbitrary twice continuously differentiable production function, we will require g to have at least $1 + (N-1+I+J) + (N-1+I+J+1)(N-1+I+J)/2$ independent parameters, and so T, the number of observations, must exceed this number. If the capital stocks k^t are truly fixed over all observations, then (82) is replaced with $x_1 = g(x_2,x_3,\ldots,x_N,s_1,\ldots,s_I)$ and we will require g to have at least $1 + (N-1+I) + (N-1+I+1)(N-1+I)/2$ independent parameters. In the variable capital stock case, if $N = I = J = 10$, we would require that T exceed

465. In the fixed capital stock case, if N = 10 = I, we would require that T exceed 210. Thus, it can be seen that even for very modest numbers of goods, it will be impossible to estimate the technology set to the second order by using the production function equation (82) alone.

The second reason why we do not recommend estimating the technology using (82) alone is related to our first reason: even if we do have enough degrees of freedom to estimate g to the second order, the resulting estimates will tend to be very unreliable due to problems of multicollinearity.

Recall that $p^t \cdot x^t = \pi(p^t, s^t, k^t)$ and consider the following system of equations, for t = 1,2,...,T:

(83) $$p^t \cdot x^t = \pi(p^t, s^t, k^t) + e_0^t$$

(84) $$x_n^t = \partial \pi(p^t, s^t, k^t)/\partial p_n + e_n^t \quad , \qquad n = 1,2,\ldots,N.$$

Equations (84) are the many period counterpart to equations (31) above; see also (15) in Appendix 1. We have added stochastic errors e_0^t and e_n^t to (83) and (84).

Since the profit function π may be used to construct the firm's technology set (see Appendix 1 for the details) and since our firm gross benefits measure defined by (2) is defined in terms of the profit function, we need only assume a differentiable functional form for π (consistent with Properties 1 and 2 defined in Appendix 1, linear homogeneity and convexity in prices) and we may use the N + 1 equations (83) and (84) (or a transformation of these equations) in order to estimate the unknown parameters of π. However, it must be noted that only N of the N+1 equations can be used in the econometric estimation procedure because $\pi(p^t, s^t, k^t) \equiv \Sigma_{n=1}^{N} p_n^t \partial\pi(p^t, s^t, k^t)/\partial p_n$ (see equation (25) in Appendix 1) and hence the error e_0^t in equation (84) is an exact linear combination of the errors in the N equations (84); i.e., $e_0^t = \Sigma_{n=1}^{N} p_n^t e_n^t$. Put another way, if all N equations (84) are estimated, equation (83) adds no new information. In any case, estimating the unknown parameters of π using N of the N + 1 equations (83) and (84) will lead to NT degrees of freedom rather than just the T degrees of freedom associated with estimating the single equation (82). This is an overwhelming advantage for the dual approach to the estimation of technology sets.

However, there are some disadvantages to the dual approach: (i) we now require data on the prices p^t, data which were not required in the production function estimation approach and (ii) we now require the hypothesis of competitive (i.e., the producer regards prices as fixed) variable profit maximizing behaviour. The production function approach required only the much weaker hypothesis of technical efficiency.

What properties should we look for in our assumed functional form for π? The following four properties seem to be desirable: (i) <u>flexibility</u>; i.e., the functional form for π has sufficient free parameters to be able to provide a second order approximation to an arbitrary twice continuously differentiable function with the appropriate a priori theoretical properties (recall equations (41) - (43) above), (ii) <u>parsimony</u>; i.e., the functional form for π has the minimal number of free parameters required to have the flexibility property, (iii) <u>linearity</u>; i.e., the unknown parameters of π appear in equations (83) and (84) in a linear fashion (this facilitates econometric estimation), and (iv) <u>consistency</u>; i.e., the functional form for π is consistent with the appropriate theoretical properties that a restricted profit function must possess (namely positive linear homogeneity and convexity in prices; see Properties 1 and 2 in Appendix 1).

Before we exhibit specific functional forms for $\pi(p,s,k)$ that may or may not be consistent with the four properties listed above, it is useful to note a result that was derived in section 3 above. If the firm faces a user charge in period t for the ith type of infrastructure service, w_i^t say, and the firm maximizes profits with respect to its utilization of service, i, then the following equation will hold (see equation i in (17) above:

$$w_i^t = \partial\pi(p^t,s^t,k^t)/\partial s_i + \varepsilon_i^t \tag{85}$$

where ε_i^t is a stochastic error term. We may now add equation (85) to our earlier estimating equations (84) for all periods t such that $s_i^t > 0$. If for some periods t, service i is not available to the firm, then $s_i^t = 0$ and we will not have an observable dependent variable w_i^t for that period.

We turn now to some possible functional forms for π.

7.2 The Translog Restricted Profit Function

In estimating the translog functional form, we use the following logarithmic transformation of (83): for $t = 1,2,\ldots,T$,

$$\begin{aligned} \ln p^t\cdot x^t = {} & a_0 + \Sigma_{n=1}^N a_n \ln p_n^t + \Sigma_{m=1}^M b_m \ln z_m^t + (1/2)\Sigma_{n=1}^N \Sigma_{i=1}^N c_{ni} \ln p_n^t \ln p_i^t \\ & + \Sigma_{n=1}^N \Sigma_{m=1}^M d_{nm} \ln p_n^t \ln z_m^t + (1/2)\Sigma_{m=1}^M \Sigma_{j=1}^M e_{mj} \ln z_m^t \ln z_j^t + e_0^t \end{aligned} \tag{86}$$

where the I infrastructure service utilization variables in period t (the s_i^t) and the J capital stock variables k_j^t are combined and written as a z^t vector, i.e., $z^t \equiv (z_1^t, z_2^t, \ldots, z_I^t, z_{I+1}^t, \ldots, z_M^t) \equiv (s_1^t, s_2^t, \ldots, s_I^t, k_1^t, \ldots, k_J^t)$ where $M \equiv I + J$ (if some of the capital variables are fixed throughout the sample period, then they are dropped from the z vector so M could be less than I + J), e_0^t is a period t stochastic error term and the a_n, b_m, c_{ni}, d_{nm}, and e_{mj} are unknown parameters to be estimated. We assume that the c_{ni} and the e_{mj} satisfy the following symmetry conditions:

$$(87) \qquad c_{ni} = c_{in} \qquad \text{for } 1 \leq n < i \leq N \text{ and}$$

$$(88) \qquad e_{mj} = e_{jm} \qquad \text{for } 1 \leq m < j \leq M.$$

When undertaking an econometric estimation using equation (86), the terms $(1/2)c_{ni}\ell np_n^t \ell p_i^t + (1/2)c_{in}\ell np_i^t \ell np_n^t$ for $i \neq n$ must be combined into the single term $c_{ni}\ell np_n^t \ell np_i^t$ for $n < i$ and the terms $(1/2)e_{mj}\ell nz_m^t \ell nz_j^t + (1/2)e_{jm}\ell nz_j^t \ell nz_m^t$ must be combined into the single term $e_{mj}\ell nz_m^t \ell nz_j^t$ for $m < j$, or else exact multicollinearity will occur.

Taking the symmetry restrictions (87) and (88) into account, there are $1 + N + M + N(N+1)/2 + NM + M(M+1)/2$ parameters on the right hand side of (86). The functional form on the right hand side of (86) (without the error term e_0^t) is defined to be $\ell n\pi(p^t, z^t)$ where $\pi(p^t, z^t)$ is defined to be the _translog restricted profit function_.

From Proposition 1 in Appendix 1, we know that $\pi(p,z)$ must be (positively) linearly homogeneous in its p variables; i.e., for $\lambda > 0$, we must have $\pi(\lambda p, z) = \lambda\pi(p,z)$. Necessary and sufficient conditions for the translog restricted profit function to have this linear homogeneity property are given by the following restrictions on the parameters which appear in (86):

(89) $\Sigma_{n=1}^{N} a_n = 1,$

(90) $\Sigma_{i=1}^{N} c_{ni} = 0$ for $n = 1,2,\ldots,N$ and

(91) $\Sigma_{n=1}^{N} d_{nm} = 0$ for $m = 1,2,\ldots,M.$

It is very easy to impose the 1 + N + M linear restrictions on the parameters which appear in (86) using RESTRICT statements using the econometrics computer program SHAZAM; see White [1978][1985].

Estimating the unknown parameters occuring in the single equation (86) will lead to the same multicollinearity and degrees of freedom problems that plagued the estimation of the production function (82). We need to use equations (84) or a transformation of them. Since $x_n^t = \partial\pi(p^t,z^t)/\partial p_n$ for $n = 1,\ldots,N$, we also have $\partial \ln\pi(p^t,z^t)/\partial \ln p_n = p_n^t x_n^t/\pi(p^t,z^t) = p_n^t x_n^t/p^t \cdot x^t$. Since the right hand side of (86) is $\ln\pi(p^t,x^t)$ (without the error term e_0^t), we may differentiate it with respect to $\ln p_n^t$ and we obtain the following system of estimating equations after adding errors e_n^t:

(92) $p_n^t x_n^t/p^t \cdot x^t = a_n + \Sigma_{i=1}^{N} c_{ni} \ln p_i^t + \Sigma_{m=1}^{M} d_{nm} \ln z_m^t + e_n^t;\ n = 1,2,\ldots,N-1.$

We do not add equation n = N to the system of N − 1 equations defined by (92) since it adds no new information to the system of estimating equations defined by (86) and (92). It is very easy to use SHAZAM to estimate the sytem of N equations (86) and (92) using a SYSTEM command. Of course, RESTRICT statements must also be used to impose the 1 + N + M linear restrictions (89) - (91) and (N-1)(1+N+M) additional restrict statements must be used in order to ensure that the parameters which occur in the N-1 equations (92) are identical to the corresponding parameters which occur in equation (86). However, the 1985 version of SHAZAM does require that the number of observations exceed the number of parameters that occur in any one equation. Since all of the parameters occur in (86), it is quite likely that this requirement will not be met in many applications, in which case a two stage Generalized Least Squares procedure will have to be used. This last procedure involves combining all N regression equations (86) and (92) into one big regression equation with NT degrees of freedom. After a preliminary big regression has been run, the sample residuals are used to form an estimated variance-covariance matrix which is then used in a Generalized Least Squares command; see White [1985] for the GLS command in SHAZAM.

The above translog restricted profit function model does rather well with respect to the theoretical criteria listed in section 7.1 above: it is <u>flexible</u>, <u>parsimonious</u>, <u>linear in the unknown parameters</u> and <u>consistent</u> with the linear homogeneity in prices property that profit functions must possess if the linear restrictions (89) - (91) are imposed. However, the translog model does have one major problem: it usually will not be globally consistent with the convexity in prices property that profit functions must possess. In fact, the econometrically estimated translog model will often not even statisfy the convexity property in neighbourhoods of the sample points. Lau [1978] and Gallant and Golub [1985] have developed numerical methods for imposing the convexity property on $\pi(p,z)$ locally, but these methods are expensive and not always satisfactory in practice.

To check whether the convexity property is satisfied locally at the sample points, calculate the matrix of second order partial derivatives with respect to prices, $\nabla^2_{pp}\pi^e(p^t,z^t)$, at each sample point and check whether the resulting matrix is positive semidefinite for $t = 1,2,\ldots,T$. The function $\ln\pi^e(p^t,z^t)$ is defined by the right hand side of (86) (omitting the error term e_0^t) where the unknown parameters a_n, b_n, etc. are replaced by their estimated values. Positive semidefiniteness of $\nabla^2_{pp}\pi^e(p^t,z^t)$ may be checked by the usual diagonalization procedure or by checking that all principal submatrices have nonnegative determinants; see Strang [1967;244] for the details of these procedures.

In addition to the possible lack of convexity problem which cannot be readily remedied, there is an additional difficulty with the translog model which can be remedied. In dealing with infrastructure services being delivered to a firm over time, it is very likely that for some services i, $s_i^t = 0$ for $t < t^*$ and $s_i^t > 0$ for $t \geq t^*$; i.e., service i is unavailable for the earlier periods in our sample of periods. In the context of applying our model to a cross section sample of firms which are in the same industry, it is even more likely that some firms are unable to utilize some types of infrastructure service so that for these firms t and those types of service i, we have $s_i^t = 0$ and hence $z_i^t = s_i^t$ equals zero also. This is rather unfortunate, since $\ln z_i^t$ appears on the right hand side of equations (86) and (92). The computer will have a great deal of difficulty in taking the natural logarithm of 0, which is, of course, equal to minus infinity.

The solution to the above problem is rather simple: if for service i and for any t, we have $z_i^t = s_i^t = 0$, then for all periods t replace z_i^t in (86) and

(92) by $1 + z_i^t$. If $z_i^t = 0$ for all periods t, then drop the variable z_i from all of the regression equations.

The above solution makes it difficult to impose a linear homogeneity property on the z variables. In Appendix 1, we show that if the firm technology set exhibits constant returns to scale (i.e., is a cone), then $\pi(p,\lambda z) = \lambda\pi(p,z)$ for all $\lambda > 0$. However, if the investigator wishes to impose a constant returns to scale property on the technology, and if one of the z_i^t variables is always positive (suppose this is so for i = M), then we suggest the following procedure: in equations (86) and (92), replace x_n^t by x_n^t/z_M^t for n = 1,2,...,N, replace z_i^t by $1 + (z_i^t/z_M^t)$ for i = 1,...,M-1, and drop the variable z_M^t so that M is replaced by M-1 in all of the summations. In this case, our estimated profit function becomes a unit scale restricted profit function and it may be used to reconstruct the firm's constant returns to scale technology set.

We turn now to another possible functional form for π.

7.3 The Biquadratic Restricted Profit Function

We define the (normalized) biquadratic restricted profit function $\pi(p,z)$ by the right hand side of the following counterpart to (83) (without the error term e_0^t):

$$(93) \qquad p^t \cdot x^t = \Sigma_{n=1}^{N} a_n p_n^t + (1/2)\Sigma_{n=1}^{N-1}\Sigma_{i=1}^{N-1} b_{ni} p_n^t p_i^t (p_N^t)^{-1} + \Sigma_{n=1}^{N}\Sigma_{m=1}^{M} c_{nm} p_n^t z_m^t + (1/2)(\Sigma_{n=1}^{N}\beta_n p_n^t)\Sigma_{m=1}^{M}\Sigma_{j=1}^{M} d_{mj} z_m^t z_j^t + e_0^t$$

$$\equiv \pi(p^t, z^t) + e_0^t$$

where we define all variables as we did for equation (86), and the a_n, b_{ni}, c_{nm} and d_{mj} are unknown parameters to be estimated. We assume that the b_{ni} and d_{mj} satisfy the following symmetry conditions:

(94) $\quad b_{ni} = b_{in} \quad$ for $1 \leq n < i \leq N$ and

(95) $\quad d_{mj} = d_{jm} \quad$ for $1 \leq m < j \leq M$.

We assume that the parameters β_n are known nonnegative numbers which are not all equal to zero. A good a priori choice for the numbers β_n is given by

(96) $\quad \beta_n \equiv 1/p_n^1 \quad$ for $n = 1,2,\ldots,N-1$ and $\beta_N \equiv 0$

where $p^1 \equiv (p_1^1,\ldots,p_N^1) \gg 0_N$ is the price vector for period 1. Another possible choice for the vector $\beta \equiv (\beta_1,\ldots,\beta_N)$ is $\beta = x^0/p^0 \cdot x^0$ where $x^0 > 0_N$ is a nonnegative, nonzero reference quantity vector and $p^0 \gg 0_N$ is an arbitrary positive reference price vector. We assume that the vector of parameters β is known a priori in order to keep the number of unknown parameters to a minimal number and also to make the right hand side of (93) linear in the unknown a_n, b_{ni}, c_{nm} and d_{mj} parameters.

In the proof of Proposition 2 in Appendix 4, we showed that the biquadratic profit function defined in (93) is a flexible functional form for a restricted profit function for <u>any</u> given $\beta > 0_N$ vector. Moreover, it is a parsimonious flexible functional form.

The system of derived net supply estimating equations (84) which corresponds to the biquadratic profit function is given by (97) and (98) below:

$$(97) \qquad x_n^t = a_n + \Sigma_{i=1}^{N-1} b_{ni} p_i^t (p_N^t)^{-1} + \Sigma_{m=1}^{M} c_{nm} z_m^t$$

$$+ (1/2)\beta_n \Sigma_{m=1}^{M} \Sigma_{j=1}^{M} d_{mj} z_m^t z_j^t + e_n^t ; \qquad n = 1,2,\ldots,N-1;$$

$$(98) \qquad x_N^t = a_n - (1/2)\Sigma_{n=1}^{N-1}\Sigma_{i=1}^{N-1} b_{ni} p_n^t p_i^t (p_N^t)^{-2} + \Sigma_{m=1}^{M} c_{Nm} z_m^t$$

$$+ (1/2)\beta_N \Sigma_{m=1}^{M} \Sigma_{j=1}^{M} d_{mj} z_m^t z_j^t + e_N^t.$$

We recommend that the system of N estimating equations given by (97) and (98) be used to estimate the unknown parameters of π; i.e., we do <u>not</u> recommend that equation (93) be used as one of our independent estimating equations, due to multicollinearity problems. We also recommend that β_N be chosen to be zero so that the number of parameters that appear in (98) is reduced to $1 + N(N-1)/2 + M$ taking the symmetry conditions (94) into account. We assume that the number of observations T is larger than $1 + N(N-1)/2 + M$. The number of parameters which appear in each of the N-1 equations in (97) is $N + M + M(M+1)/2$; we asume that T is larger than this number also.

A SYSTEM command in SHAZAM may be used to estimate all of the unknown parameters which occur in (97) and (98) in a simultaneous fashion. It will be necessary to collect the terms $(1/2)\ \beta_n d_{mj} z_m^t z_j^t$ and $(1/2)\beta_n d_{jm} z_j^t z_m^t$ into one term, $\beta_n d_{mj} z_j^t\ z_m^t$, for $1 \leq m < j \leq M$. Also, many RESTRICT statements will have to be used to ensure that all parameters b_{ni} and d_{mj} that appear in more than one equation are restricted to be the same in the final result. We leave the rather messy details to the reader.

If the firm faces the user fee $w_i^t > 0$ for the ith type of infrastructure service in period t and the profit maximizing firm is utilizing a positive amount of this type of service during period t so that $s_i^t = z_i^t > 0$, then we may add the following estimating equation to the system (97) and (98) to aid in the estimation of the unknown parameters (recall (85) above):

$$(99) \qquad w_i^t = \Sigma_{n=1}^{N} c_{ni} p_n^t + (\Sigma_{n=1}^{N} \beta_n p_n^t) \Sigma_{m=1}^{M} d_{mi} z_m^t + \varepsilon_i^t.$$

RESTRICT statements will have to be used to ensure that the c_{ni} and d_{mi} which appear in (99) are equal to the corresponding parameters which occur in (97) and (98).

It is easy to verify that the biquadratic profit function $\pi(p,t)$ defined by (93) has the required linear homogeneity in prices property. We can check whether the required convexity in prices property is satisfied at the sample points by calculating the matrix of second order partial derivatives of π with respect to prices, $\nabla^2_{pp}\pi(p^t,z^t)$, and then checking whether the matrix is positive semidefinite or not. It can be verified that the second order derivatives of π are given by the following formulae:

$$(100) \qquad \partial^2\pi(p^t,z^t)/\partial p_i \partial p_j = b_{ij}(p_N^t)^{-1}, \qquad 1 \leq i,\ j \leq N-1:$$

$$(101) \qquad \partial^2\pi(p^t,z^t)/\partial p_N \partial p_j = \Sigma_{i=1}^{N-1} b_{ij} p_i^t (p_N^t)^{-2}, \qquad j = 1,2,\ldots,N-1;$$

$$(102) \qquad \partial^2\pi(p^t,z^t)/\partial p_N \partial p_N = \Sigma_{i=1}^{N-1}\Sigma_{j=1}^{N-1} b_{ij} p_i^t p_j^t (p_N^t)^{-3}.$$

Using the linear homogeneity of $\pi(p,z)$ in its p variables, it can be verified (see equations (28) and (29) in Appendix 1) that $|\nabla_{pp}^2\pi(p^t,z^t)| = 0$; i.e., the determinant of the N by N matrix of second order partial derivatives of $\pi(p^t,z^t)$ with respect to the components of p must be zero. Hence, using the necessary and sufficient determinantal conditions for checking whether $\nabla_{pp}^2\pi(p^t,z^t)$ is positive semidefinite or not (see Strang [1976;244] for these conditions), it can be seen that we need only check whether the submatrix of $\nabla_{pp}^2\pi(p^t,z^t)$, which deletes the last row and column of $\nabla_{pp}^2\pi(p^t,v^t)$, is positive semidefinite or not. This N-1 by N-1 submatrix is equal to $(p_N^t)^{-1}B$ where $B \equiv [b_{ij}]$ is the N-1 by N-1 matrix of the b_{ij} parameters which occur in the definition of π, (93). Hence, if the econometrically estimated B matrix is positive semidefinite, then the estimated biquadratic profit function will satisfy the required convexity in prices property for all $p \gg 0_N$ and $z \geq 0_M$; i.e., it will satisfy the convexity property globally.

By Proposition 3 in Appendix 1, it was shown that if the underlying firm production possibilities set T^f is convex, then the corresponding restricted profit function $\pi(p,z)$ will be concave in the components of z. We can check whether our estimated biquadratic restricted profit function satisfies this concavity property at the sample points by computing the matrix of second order partial derivatives of π with respect to the components of z,$\nabla_{zz}^2\pi(p^t,z^t)$, and then checking whether this matrix is negative semidefinite, or not. The required second order derivatives of π are given by:

(103) $\partial^2\pi(p^t,z^t)/\partial z_i\partial z_j = (\Sigma_{n=1}^{N}\beta_n p_n^t)d_{ij}$, $1 \le i, j \le M$.

Thus the M by M matrix of second order derivatives is given by $\nabla^2_{zz}\pi(p^t,z^t) = (\Sigma_{n=1}^{N}\beta_n p_n^t)D$ where $D \equiv [d_{ij}]$ is the M by M matrix of the d_{ij} parameters which occur in the definition of π, (93). Since $\Sigma_{n=1}^{N}\beta_n p_n^t > 0$ for all $p^t \gg 0_N$, it can be seen that if the econometrically estimated D matrix is negative semidefinite, then the estimated biquadratic profit function $\pi(p,z)$ will be concave in the components of z for all $p \gg 0_N$ and $z \ge 0_M$.

Now suppose that the estimated B matrix is not positive semidefinite. Then we may reverse our reasoning above and conclude that our estimated biquadratic profit function does not satisfy the required convexity in prices property anywhere. What can we do in this situation?

We suggest the use of the following technique, due to Wiley, Schmidt and Bramble [1973;318]: reparameterize the matrix B by replacing it by the product of a lower triangular square matrix of dimension N-1 by N-1, A say, times its transpose, A^T; i.e, set

(104) $B = AA^T$; $A \equiv [a_{ij}]$, $i,j = 1,\ldots,N-1$; $a_{ij} = 0$ for $i < j$.

Using a representation theorem due to Lau [1978;427], Diewert and Wales [1984] show that the above reparameterization technique is a perfectly general method for restricting B to be positive semidefinite. Notice that in view of the symmetry restrictions (94) on the elements of B, replacing the b_{ij} parameters by the a_{ij} parameters does not change the total number of parameters to be estimated using equations (97) and (98). However, our suggested reparameterization procedure is far from being costless: we must now use nonlinear rather than linear (or iterative linear) regression techniques, and the costs of estimating the model will rise considerably.

Obviously, a similar technique may be used in order to impose negative semidefiniteness on the D matrix: replace D by $-EE^T$ where E is a lower triangular matrix of size M by M. However, since there is no necessity for $\pi(p,z)$ to be concave in z, we do not recommend that the investigator undertake the above replacement of D by $-EE^T$ unless there are very good reasons for doing so.

Suppose the investigator wishes to impose constant returns to scale on the technology. Then from Proposition 4 in Appendix 1, $\pi(p,z)$ must be linearly homogeneous in its z arguments, i.e., we have $\pi(p,\lambda z) = \lambda\pi(p,z)$ for all $\lambda > 0$, $z \geq 0_M$ and $p \gg 0_N$. Obviously, the biquadratic profit function defined by (93) cannot satisfy this homogeneity property. Assuming that $z_M^t > 0$ for $t = 1,2,\ldots,T$, we may adapt our biquadratic model to the constant returns to scale case as follows: in (93), (97), (98) and (99), replace x_n^t by x_n^t/z_M^t, replace z_m^t by z_m^t/z_M^t for $m = 1,2,\ldots,M-1$ and change the index M to M-1. Perform the econometric estimation using the new system (97), (98) and possibly (99), and we obtain our estimated unit scale biquadratic restricted profit function, $\tilde{\pi}(p,z_1/z_M,\ldots,z_{M-1}/z_M)$ say, involving only M-1 transformed $\tilde{z}_m = z_m/z_M$ arguments. The overall restricted profit function may now be defined in terms of $\tilde{\pi}$ as follows: $\pi(p,z_1,\ldots,z_M) \equiv \tilde{\pi}(p,z_1/z_M,\ldots,z_{M-1}/z_M)z_M$.

We conclude this section by examining how the biquadratic restricted profit function defined in (93) does with respect to the theoretical criteria listed in section 7.1 above: it is flexible, parsimonious, linear in the unknown parameters, and consistent with the linear homogeneity in prices property that functions must possess. Moreover, if the estimated $B = [b_{ij}]$

matrix is positive semidefinite, then the estimated profit function satisfies the convexity in prices property that profit functions must possess <u>globally</u>. Finally, if the estimated B matrix is not positive semidefinite, then the Wiley, Schmidt and Bramble reparameterization procedure may be used to impose the convexity in prices property in a way that will not destroy the flexibility of the functional form. However, the cost of this reparameterization procedure is that the model is no longer linear in the unknown parameters, so that nonlinear regression techniques have to be used.

At this point, it appears that the biquadratic profit function has a clear advantage over the translog profit function studies in 7.2 above, since the former model may satisfy the convexity in prices property globally if we are lucky and the estimated B matrix turns out to be positive semidefinite. Even if we are unlucky and the estimated B matrix turns out not to be positive semidefinite, we may readily impose the convexity property globally, whereas in the translog case, the convexity property is imposed locally and there is no guarantee that global convexity will prevail.

However, the biquadratic functional form does suffer from one disadvantage that is not shared by the translog functional form: the former functional form is not symmetric in its p variables; i.e., we have asymmetrically singled out good N to play the role of a price deflator in (93). Hence, different choices for this numeraire good will lead to different functional forms for π. All of these functional forms will be flexible, but in practice, they may fit the data rather differently and give rise to rather different patterns of elasticities. Hence, the investigator may well have difficulty in deciding which good to choose as the numeraire good.

Notes

For additional material on functional form problems in production theory, see Diewert [1974], Lau [1974][1984b], Fuss, McFadden and Mundlak [1978], McFadden [1978], Barnett [1983], and Jorgenson [1984b]. The concepts of flexibility, parsimony and linearity may be found in Diewert [1969][1971]; the term "flexible" is due to Diewert [1974;113] and the term "parsimonious" is due to Fuss, McFadden and Mundlak [1978].

The translog functional form was first introduced as a functional form for a production or cost function by Christensen, Jorgenson and Lau [1971]; see Jorgenson [1984b] for a detailed bibliography of translog cost function applications. The translog restricted profit function was introduced by Diewert [1974;139] and Russell and Boyce [1974].

Jorgenson and Fraumeni [1981] utilize a method for imposing the correct curvature conditions (e.g. the convexity in prices condition that a profit function must satisfy) on a translog functional form; see also Jorgenson [1984b] for further discussion. Their method imposes the correct curvature conditions globally, but at the cost of maintaining flexibility.

Lau [1984] proves that it is impossible for a flexible, parsimonius, linear in parameters functional form for a profit function $\pi(p,z)$ to exist which is also convex, linearly homogeneous and nondecreasing in the components of p for all $p \gg 0_N$. Our suggested functional form in section 7.3 does not contradict Lau's Theorem since we do not require the global nondecreasing in p property.

Much of our discussion in section 7.3 was adapted from Diewert and Wales [1984] where the function $g(p) \equiv (1/2)\Sigma_{i=1}^{N-1}\Sigma_{n=1}^{N-1} b_{in}p_ip_np_N^{-1}$ was used to develop flexible functional forms for cost functions. The Wiley, Schmidt and Bramble

[1973] reparameterization technique was empirically implemented in Diewert and Wales.

Detailed discussions on alternative stochastic specifications for the errors in our suggested regression models can be found in Fuss, McFadden and Mundlak [1978] and Griliches [1984].

8. The Selection and Measurement of Variables in the Econometric Approach

8.1 The Measurement of Outputs

Our goal is to decompose each set of values for a firm into its price and quantity parts. We assume that our data source is a set of annual (or quarterly) accounting reports for a firm or a set of government census surveys.

We assume that in period t, p_n^t and x_n^t are the price and quantity produced of good n by the firm. The price p_n^t is a before sales tax price; i.e., it corresponds to the revenue received by the firm for selling one unit of good n during period t. The value of sales of good n in period t, v_n^t, is invariably given. For reasonably homogeneous outputs (such as cement, beer, board feet of lumber, tons of metal, etc.), quantities produced, $x_n^t > 0$, will also be given. In this case, define the corresponding price to be $p_n^t \equiv v_n^t/x_n^t > 0$; i.e., we deflate the value by the appropriate quantity.

If quantity data for good n are not available, the investigator will be forced to go to an official government source and obtain a price index p_n^t which seems to be most relevant to deflate the value. In this case, define the period t quantity of good n to be $x_n^t \equiv v_n^t/p_n^t$; i.e., we deflate the value series by the price series to form an implicit quantity series.

If we are dealing with a cross section sample of firms producing a homogeneous product, then presumably quantity information x_n^f in addition to sales information v_n^f for firm f will be available, and we calculate the firm f implicit price to be $p_n^f \equiv v_n^f/x_n^f$. Thus in the cross sectional context, the time superscript is replaced by the firm superscript f. If our cross sectional sample consists of data from different countries, then if the biquadratic model is estimated using only equations (97) and (98), it is not necessary to use exchange rates to deflate all country data into homogeneous world prices since only relative prices appear in equations (97) and (98). However if equations (99) are also used in the estimation, or if the translog model is used, then it will be useful to use exchange rates to express all prices in a common currency, since this should reduce heteroskedasticity problems.

8.2 The Measurement of Intermediate Inputs

Intermediate inputs are firm purchases of goods and services (other than labour) which are used up during the period in question, such as fuel, electricity, water, raw materials and all types of manufactured goods which are further processed or assembled by the firm. Note that some of the firm's purchases of intermediate inputs will be classified as purchases of infrastructure services $s_i^t \geq 0$ in period t and the corresponding user fee in period t is $w_i^t > 0$. We denote the negative of the firm's noninfrastructure services intermediate input purchases of good n in period t by $x_n^t < 0$ and the corresponding period t price by $p_n^t > 0$. The prices w_i^t and p_n^t include any taxes that are paid by the firm to the government for the use of the intermediate input. Note that in the case of inputs, we include sales taxes in the price of the good, while in the case of outputs, we exclude sales taxes paid by other firms or consumers from the price of the good. However, subsidies for the production of an output should be put into a per unit output basis and included in the price of the output. The general principle which should guide the researcher is to try to use the prices for inputs and outputs that the firm actually faces.

In dealing with the accounting data of a firm, the same general techniques that were used in the construction of output series may be used. If expenditures on a class of infrastructure intermediate inputs of type i during period t are v_i^t and the period t quantity utilized is $s_i^t > 0$, then define $w_i^t = v_i^t/s_i^t > 0$. If the expenditure v_i^t is not broken down into its price and quantity components, then it will be necessary to get an external price index series w_i^t and then define the corresponding period t quantity as $s_i^t = v_i^t/w_i^t > 0$. Similar techniques may be used to decompose expenditures on noninfrastructure intermediate inputs into their price and quantity components, p_n^t and x_n^t. The only difference is that the researcher must remember to measure the resulting quantity as a negative amount; i.e., we require that $x_n^t < 0$.

Unfortunately, it is often the case that the annual or quarterly financial reports of a firm will not give much detail on the firm's utilization of intermediate inputs. However, if the period t cost of sales is given, then the firm's expenditures on labour can be subtracted from this cost of sales figure to give us an implicit period t expenditure v_n^t on intermediate inputs. The researcher can then pick the most appropriate price index p_n^t to construct an implicit aggregate intermediate input quantity for period t, $x_n^t = -v_n^t/p_n^t$. This is not a very satisfactory solution to the problem of measuring accurately the firm's utilization of intermediate inputs but it may be the best we can do using only data from the annual financial reports of the firm.

8.3 The Measurement of Labour

Ideally, the firm's utilization of labour should be broken down into many micro occupational and skill categories and we should be able to collect accurate price and quantity information on each category. In reality, most firm accounting data and most census and government survey data will provide information on at most two classes of labour: production workers and administrative workers (or nonproduction workers). Let $q_n^t > 0$ be the number of workers of type n during period t and let $v_n^t > 0$ be expenditures on that class of labour for period t. Then we may define our price and quantity variables for this type of labour by $p_n^t \equiv v_n^t/q_n^t$ and $x_n^t \equiv -q_n^t < 0$ (remember, variable inputs are always indexed with a negative sign in our first class of N goods).

We should include in the expenditures v_n^t any unemployment insurance or social security payments made by the firm to the government associated with that class of worker. Any pension or other fringe benefits should also be included in v_n^t. Finally, if data on hours worked are available, it should be used in place of q_n^t, the number of workers. Even if hours worked data are not available, the investigator should try to make crude adjustments to q_n^t to reflect the long term decline in average hours worked and the increase in paid holidays and in weeks of vacation.

If overtime work is significant and (unionized) workers are paid a premium wage for their hours of overtime, then hours of overtime should be treated as a separate class of labour and we should construct separate wage and quantity series for these classes of overtime labour, if the data permit this. For other measurement problems that occur when measuring labour services from the viewpoint of production theory, see Triplett [1983].

8.4 The Measurement of Inventories of Goods in Process

Many firms hold substantial inventories of raw materials and partially finished products during the accounting period under consideration. These average stocks of goods in process facilitate the production of the firm's final outputs, and hence they should be considered a factor of production, just like the firm's utilization of labour or its consumption of electricity. However, an average stock of inventories held during the period differs from the firm's consumption of electricity, since at the end of the current period, the average stock of inventories is available for use during the following period; i.e., the inventory input is a *durable* input rather than a *nondurable* one.

The existence of durable inputs in the production process leads to significant difficulties in measuring the contribution of the services of that durable input to the current period. If we are attempting to find an econometric approximation to a firm's one period (static) production possibilities set (or to its dual restricted profit function) as opposed to approximating an intertemporal production possibilities set as in section 5.1

above then it is clear that we cannot simply charge to the current period the entire purchase cost of a new unit of a durable input, since the durable good will also yield services in future periods.

One way of proceeding is to specialize our general Hicksian intertemporal user cost formula (49) to the present situation. Suppose that variable good n is an inventory durable good and that the observable spot price for one unit of the good purchased in period t by the firm is $\tilde{p}_n^t > 0$. Suppose further that the firm manager in period t <u>expects</u> the period t+1 spot price for the durable to be $P_n^t \geq 0$ and that the relevant opportunity cost of capital that the firm faces in period t is $r_t > -1$. (If the firm is borowing in period t, r_t is the firm's marginal borrowing rate; if the firm is lending funds in period t out of its cash flow, then r_t is the interest rate on the last loan made.) Under these conditions, the firm's <u>expected user cost</u> p_n^t for good n in period t will be equal to the cost of purchasing one unit of the durable good in period t minus the discounted expected resale value of the good in the following period; i.e., we have

$$(105) \qquad p_n^t \equiv \tilde{p}_n^t - (1+r_t)^{-1} P_n^t$$

$$(106) \qquad = [r_t\tilde{p}_n^t - (P_n^t - \tilde{p}_n^t)]/(1+r_t) \ .$$

The rearrangement of (105) that is given by (106) reflects the fact that the user cost may be decomposed into a nominal interest payments term, $r_t\tilde{p}_n^t/(1+r_t)$, and the negative of the expected capital gains term, $(P_n^t-\tilde{p}_n^t)/(1+r_t)$, which can offset the interest payments term.

The user cost formula (105) has two measurement difficulties that did not occur until now: (i) we now have to worry about the firm's financial status in order to determine the correct opportunity cost of capital r_t and (ii) we have to guess what the firm expects next period's price to be. It is not in general appropriate to use next period's actual spot price $\tilde{p}_n^{t+1}$ in place of this period's expectation of what that spot price will be, P_n^t, since we are implicitly assuming that the firm cannot sell a unit of inventory purchased in period t until period t+1. Hence the firm's actual ex post user cost, $\tilde{p}_n^t - (1+r_t)^{-1}\tilde{p}_n^{t+1}$, cannot be known to the firm until after the decision to hold the good through period t has been made. The firm's decision whether to hold a unit of good n through period t or not must be made on the basis of the unobservable ex ante user cost defined by (105). Moreover, the use of ex post user costs in place of the ex ante user cost defined by (105) will frequently lead the econometric investigator into severe difficulties: in times of rapid inflation, ex post capital gains on durable goods will often be greater than nominal interest rates and so ex post user costs will become negative and our econometric model based on profit maximizing behavior will not make sense. Hence in periods of rapid inflation, the investigator may be forced to construct an econometric rational expectations forecasting model to form forecasts for P_n^t. Alternatively, a relatively crude ad hoc moving average forecasting scheme could be used; e.g., assume that next period's percentage increase in price is a weighted average of the price increases that occurred in the last three periods.

If inflation has been moderate during the sample period, then it may be acceptable to assume static expectations; i.e., assume that next period's expected spot price P_n^t is equal to this period's spot price $\tilde{p}_n^t$. In this case, the user cost formula (105) becomes

$$(107) \qquad p_n^t = r_t \tilde{p}_n^t/(1+r_t).$$

Unfortunately, our measurement difficulties in dealing with inventories and other durable goods are not yet over. In most countries, firms pay business or corporation income taxes. If the firm did not purchase any durable goods, then in many countries, the firm's tax liability would just be equal to its profits and it would pay a business income tax equal to say τ times its profits where $0 < \tau < 1$. Under these conditions, the business income tax would not affect our firm profit maximization models (1) and (18); i.e., the business income tax would be <u>neutral</u>. However, when a firm purchases durable goods such as inventories, the tax treatment of these purchases is generally different and it does affect our firm profit maximization models, as we shall now demonstrate.

Rather than introducing a separate notation to distinguish between nondurable goods and inventory durables, we allow the possibility that all of our N variable goods could be inventory durables. The vector of period t spot prices is now $\tilde{p}^t \equiv (\tilde{p}_1^t, \tilde{p}_2^t, \ldots, \tilde{p}_N^t)$ and the period t vector of spot prices for durables that are <u>expected</u> to prevail in period t+1 is $P^t \equiv (P_1^t, P_2^t, \ldots, P_N^t)$. If good n is a nondurable good, then we define $P_n^t \equiv 0$. Assuming as before that r_t is the relevant opportunity cost of capital in period t and that the relevant income tax rate is τ, the firm's period t static profit maximization problem is no longer (1) but the following problem:

$$(108) \qquad \max_x \{\tilde{p}^t \cdot x - (1+r_t)^{-1}P^t \cdot x - \tau[p^t \cdot x - D^t \cdot x] : (x,s^f,k^f)\varepsilon T^f\}$$

where $D^t \equiv (D_1^t, D_2^t, \ldots, D_N^t)$ and $\tilde{p}_n^t - D_n^t$ is the per unit amount the firm is allowed to deduct from its period t taxable income for each unit of good n purchased by the firm during period t (if good n is a nondurable, define $D_n^t \equiv 0$). The first two terms in the objective function of (108) correspond to the sum $p^t \cdot x \equiv \Sigma_{n=1}^N p_n^t x_n$ where the old user cost of good n with no business taxes is p_n^t defined by (105). The term in square brackets in the objective function for (108) corresponds to taxable income in period t. By rearranging terms, we may rewrite (108) as follows:

$$\max_x\{(1-\tau)[\tilde{p}^t \cdot x - (1-\tau)^{-1}(1+r_t)^{-1}P^t \cdot x + (1-\tau)^{-1}\tau D^t \cdot x : (x,s^f,k^f)\varepsilon T^f]$$

$$(109) \qquad = (1-\tau)\max_x\{[\tilde{p}^t - (1-\tau)^{-1}(1+r_t)^{-1}P^t + (1-\tau)^{-1}\tau D^t] \cdot x : (x,s^f,k^f)\varepsilon T^f\}$$

$$\equiv (1-\tau)\pi^f(\tilde{p}^t - (1-\tau)^{-1}(1+r_t)^{-1}P^t + (1-\tau)^{-1}\tau D^t, s^f, k^f)$$

where the equality (109) follows using the definition of the firm f restricted profit function π^f defined by (1). Define the vector of period t <u>user costs</u> when there is a business income tax to be $p^t \equiv (p_1^t, \ldots, p_N^t)$ and define component n to be

$$(110) \qquad p_n^t \equiv \tilde{p}_n^t - (1-\tau)^{-1}(1+r_t)^{-1}P_n^t + (1-\tau)^{-1}\tau D_n^t \quad , \quad n = 1,2,\ldots,N.$$

Of course, if good n is a nondurable, then we define $P_n^t \equiv 0$, $D_n^t \equiv 0$ and $p_n^t = \tilde{p}_n^t$; the period t user cost equals the period t spot price.

Comparing (109) with (110), we see that p_n^t defined by (110) is the appropriate period t price for good n that should be used in our econometric model. It can be seen that the user cost formula for a durable inventory good with income taxes, (110), is considerably more complex than the user cost formula without taxes, (105).

Formula (110) can be simplified if we are willing to make some heroic assumptions. If good n is a durable and the government sets $D_n^t = (1+r_t)^{-1}P_n^t$, so that the government uses the same prices to compute the firm's period t taxable income as the firm uses in its objective function in the no tax situation, then (110) reduces to (105). Alternatively, if we assume that the firm expects that the current period t price of the durable inventory good n will persist into the next period so that $P_n^t = \tilde{p}_n^t$ and we assume that the government sets $D_n^t = (1+r_t)^{-1}\tilde{p}_n^t$, then (110) collapses down to (107). Finally, we could assume that the firm anticipates next period's spot price for the inventory good n perfectly so that $P_n^t = \tilde{p}_n^{t+1}$ and the government sets $D_n^t = (1+r_t)^{-1}\tilde{p}_n^{t+1}$. Under these circumstances, the user cost for inventory good n becomes

$$(111) \qquad p_n^t = \tilde{p}_n^t - (1+r_t)^{-1}\tilde{p}_n^{t+1}.$$

(If good n is a nondurable good, then we still set $p_n^t = \tilde{p}_n^t$.) Formula (111) corresponds to a perfect anticipations model with cash flow taxation.

None of the above special cases of the general formula (110) are very satisfactory. However, the existence of durable inventory inputs creates significant measurement problems in the econometric approach to production theory, and we do not have any universally valid suggestions for dealing with these problems.

8.5 The Measurement of Capital Stock Components

There are a number of alternative approaches to the measurement of a firm's capital stock components and we will outline several of them.

The first method we shall discuss is Jorgenson's vintage accounts method (see Jorgenson [1963], Christensen and Jorgenson [1973] and Jorgenson [1984b]).

We assume that the firm uses the services of J durable capital stock inputs during each period. We denote the quantity of the jth capital good purchased by the firm in period t by $I_j^t \geq 0$ and we assume that the price of one unit of this good in period t is $Q_j^t > 0$. Thus the period t expenditures on the jth class of capital goods is $V_j^t \equiv Q_j^t I_j^t$ for $j = 1,2,\ldots,J$ and $t = 1,2,\ldots,T$. Usually, firm balance sheets and government surveys will have information only on the values V_j^t. In this case, it will be necessary for the researcher to find appropriate price indexes Q_j^t, in order to deflate the nominal investment values V_j^t into real investment quantities I_j^t; i.e., we define

$$(112) \qquad I_j^t \equiv V_j^t / Q_j^t \quad ; \quad j = 1,\ldots,J \; ; \; t = 1,\ldots,T \, .$$

It will be advisable for the researcher to attempt to carry out the above deflation process for periods t which precede the periods for which a complete set of data has been collected and for which one of the econometric models described in the previous section is to be estimated. However, eventually the researcher will have to stop this search for ancient data on investment expenditures. At this point, it is necessary to have starting values for the different components of the capital stock. We assume that in period 1, we can obtain data on the firm's beginning of the period book value of the capital stock components, B_j^0 say, for $j = 1,2,\ldots,J$. We assume also that our capital stock component price indexes are available for the period immediately preceding period 1, Q_j^0 say for $j = 1,\ldots,J$. We then define the firm's starting capital stock for component j to be

$$(113) \qquad k_j^0 \equiv B_j^0/Q_j^0 \quad ; \quad j = 1,\ldots,J \ .$$

We now assume that one unit of an investment good of type j purchased in period 1 is <u>perfectly</u> <u>substitutable</u> with a unit of k_j. However, we assume that the <u>efficiency</u> of a unit of the period 0 capital stock has declined to $(1 - \delta_j)$ times the efficiency of a new unit of the capital stock purchased in period 1, where $0 \leq \delta_j < 1$ is the <u>depreciation</u> <u>rate</u> for the jth class of capital good. Thus in period 1, the total number of units of capital stock j, in constant efficiency units, is $k_j^1 \equiv (1-\delta_j)k_j^0 + I_j^1$. We continue this scheme for period 2, and define the total number of units of capital stock j in constant efficiency units to be $k_j^2 \equiv (1-\delta_j)k_j^1 + I_j^2 = (1-\delta_j)^2 k_j^0 + (1-\delta_j)I^1 + I_j^2$. In general, we define the capital stock in constant efficiency units for class j in period t to be

$$(114)\qquad k_j^t \equiv (1-\delta_j)^t k_j^0 + (1-\delta_j)^{t-1} I_j^1 + \ldots + (1-\delta_j) I_j^{t-1} + I_j^t \;;\; t=1,\ldots,T; \; j=1,\ldots,J.$$

The type of efficiency decline in investment goods that has been assumed in constructing the period t capital stocks k_j^t using (114) is called a declining balance or geometric pattern of efficiency decline. Other patterns of efficiency decline could be assumed but the geometric scheme has the advantage of being simple as well as being consistent with econometric evidence on actual efficiency declines; see Hulten and Wykoff [1981]. Typically, estimates for the depreciation rates of δ_j run between 7 1/2% to 33% for items of producer durable equipment and between 1 1/2% to 6% for classes of nonresidential structures; see Hulten and Wykoff [1981] or Jorgenson [1984b]. For classes of land, we would generally assume that the corresponding $\delta_j = 0$.

The above method for constructing capital stocks is a reasonable one but the researcher should keep in mind that it does impose strong a priori restrictions on the pattern of substitution between investment goods of different vintages; i.e., we are assuming that investment goods in class j of different vintages are additively separable; see Blackorby, Primont and Russell [1978] for characterizations of additive separability or complete strict separability in their terminology. We can explain the restrictive nature of (114) as follows. A general representation of the firm's one period technology set in period t is given by the dual restricted profit function, $\pi^t(p_1^t,\ldots,p_N^t;\; s_1^t,\ldots,s_I^t;\; k_1^0,\ldots,k_J^0;\; I_1^1,\ldots,I_J^1;\; I_1^2,\ldots,I_J^2;\ldots;\; I_1^t,\ldots,I_J^t)$, where the $p_n^t > 0$ are the variable good prices that the producer faces in period t, the $s_i^t \geq 0$ are the firm's period t utilizations of the various types of infrastructure services, $k^0 \equiv (k_1^0,\ldots,k_J^0) \geq 0_J$ is the firm's vector of initial starting capital stocks and $I^r \equiv (I_1^r,\ldots,I_J^r) \geq 0_J$ for $r = 1,2,\ldots,t$ is the firm's vector of purchases of investment goods in period r. In this general formulation of the producer's technology set in period t, we allow each investment good j of each vintage r, I_j^r, to enter the structure of production in an independent way; we do not restrict the substitutability of I_j^r with I_j^t for $r < t$ in any restrictive a priori manner. When we assume (114), we are assuming that the general period t profit function,

$$(115) \qquad \pi^t(p^t,s^t,k^0,I^1,\ldots,I^t) = \pi(p^t,s^t,k^t) ,$$

where $p^t \equiv (p_1^t,\ldots,p_N^t)$, $s^t \equiv (s_1^t,\ldots,s_I^t)$, $k^t \equiv (k_1^t,\ldots,k_J^t)$ and the k_j^t are defined by (114). This is a tremendous reduction in dimensionality. In the case where we have the general period t profit function, we define the relative efficiency in the period t technology set of an investment good j purchased during period $\beta \leq t$ relative to an investment good j purchased during period $\alpha < \beta$ as the partial derivative of π^t with respect to I_j^β divided by the partial derivative of π^t with respect to I_j^α; i.e.,

$$(116) \qquad d_{t,j}^{\alpha,\beta} \equiv [\partial\pi^t(p^t,s^t,k^0,I^1,\ldots,I^t)/\partial I_j^\beta]/[\partial\pi^t(p^t,s^t,k^0,I^1,\ldots,I^t)/\partial I_j^\alpha]$$
$$\text{for } j = 1,2,\ldots,J \; ; \; 1 \leq \alpha < \beta \leq t.$$

Thus the relative efficiency $d_{t,j}^{\alpha,\beta}$ will in general be a complicated function of all of the arguments, p^t, s^t, k^0, $I^1,\ldots,I^t$. Now suppose that we make the simplifying hypothesis (114) so that (115) holds. Under these conditions, the relative efficiency functions defined by (116) collapse to the constants defined by (117); i.e., we have under (114),

$$(117) \qquad d_{t,j}^{\alpha,\beta} = (1-\delta_j)^{\alpha-\beta} \quad ; \quad j = 1,\ldots,J \; ; \; 1 \leq \alpha \leq \beta \leq t.$$

Even if assumptions (114) are restrictive from the a priori point of view, we are forced to make restrictive assumptions somewhere since we cannot hope to estimate econometrically the parameters of the general period t restricted profit function, $\pi^t(p^t,s^t,k^0,I^1,\ldots,I^t)$, with its very large (and growing over time) number of arguments. Thus we do not reject the additively separable model defined by (114); we just want to caution the researcher who uses this method that its validity can be questioned.

Is there a practical alternative to using (114)? We believe that there is, but we must caution the reader that our suggested alternative method for aggregating capital has its difficulties as well. Our alternative to the additive separability approach to aggregating capital is to generalize the user cost approach to inventories to cover the general capital goods case.

We now develop the user cost counterpart to (105). Let $Q_j^t > 0$ be the purchase price for one unit of a new investment good or durable input of class j in period t (recall that we defined Q_j^t above). We assume that the firm production manager in period t expects that the resale price of the investment good j will be P_j^t in period t+1. Note that the expected price P_j^t combines the expected deterioration or depreciation of the good with any anticipated capital gain. Assuming that the firm's opportunity cost of capital in period t is r_t and that there are no business income taxes (or a system of cash flow business taxes), then the firm's expected user cost in period t for using one unit of a newly purchased investment good of type j will be

$$(118) \qquad p_j^t \equiv Q_j^t - (1+r_t)^{-1} P_j^t$$

$$(119) \qquad = [r_t Q_j^t - (P_j^t - Q_j^t)]/(1+r_t) \; ; \; j = 1,\ldots,J \; ; \; t = 1,\ldots,T.$$

The formulae (118) and (119) are exact counterparts to (105) and (106). However, now the term $P_j^t - Q_j^t$ is not a pure capital gains term. If we note that Q_j^{t+1} is the market price of a new unit of investment good j to be sold in period t+1, we may rewrite $P_j^t - Q_j^t$ as $Q_j^{t+1} - Q_j^t - [Q_j^{t+1} - P_j^t]$. The term $Q_j^{t+1} - P_j^t$ represents the expected decline in the value of the asset due to deterioration, while the term $Q_j^{t+1} - Q_j^t$ represents capital gains.

The logic behind the derivation of the user cost formula (118) for new investment goods purchased during period t can be extended to cover the case where the firm is still holding old units of investment goods during period t. We let $Q_j^{t,\alpha}$ denote the period t market price for one unit of capital good j purchased by the firm $\alpha \geq 0$ periods ago. Define $P_j^{t,\alpha}$ to be the firm's expectation for the market price next period for one unit of capital good j purchased α periods ago. If r_t denotes the firm's opportunity cost of capital in period t, then the period t <u>ex ante user cost</u> for one unit of capital good j purchased α periods ago is defined to be

$$(120) \qquad p_j^{t,\alpha} \equiv Q_j^{t,\alpha} - (1+r_t)^{-1} P_j^{t,\alpha} \quad ; \; j = 1,\ldots,J \; ; \; t = 1,\ldots,T \; ; \; 0 \leq \alpha \leq t.$$

The user cost formula (120) can be extended to cover the case where there is a business income tax. We end up with a formula similar to (110) with some obvious changes in notation.

There are a number of problems with the user cost formula (120) (and the generalized counterpart to (110)): (i) Certain classes of capital are truly fixed and cannot be readily resold. These classes of capital good should be treated as in (114). (ii) Second hand markets may not exist for many classes of investment good. (iii) Even if second hand markets do exist, it will be difficult to obtain information on the vintage prices $Q_j^{t,\alpha}$. Government statistical agencies are reluctant to provide information on the prices of second hand durables (both on the consumer and producer sides) and firm balance sheets will not provide information on relevant second hand asset prices, unless a used investment good is actually sold during the accounting period. Hence the econometric investigator will have difficulty in obtaining estimates for the $Q_j^{t,\alpha}$. Note that this lack of information problem is not as severe in the inventories case, since all "vintages" of inventory purchases can be treated as being homogeneous. (iv) We have the same problems in attempting to guess at the producer's anticipated prices $P_j^{t,\alpha}$ that we encountered in attempting to determine the firm's anticipated next period inventory prices P_n^t that occurred in (105). Actually, our problems are now more severe, because our old static expectations assumption, $P_n^t = \tilde{p}_n^t$, is not tenable in the present situation; i.e. we cannot simply assume that $P_j^{t,\alpha} = Q_j^{t,\alpha}$, because this neglects the depreciation and deterioration that the asset will be subject to under normal conditions. (v) The user cost approach requires information on interest rates r_t, on the tax rate τ, and on depreciation allowances for tax purposes; recall the D_n^t which occurred in (110).

With all of the above disadvantages, are there any advantages to the user cost approach over the additive separability approach? The main advantage of the user cost approach to the treatment of capital is that we gain degrees of freedom for our econometric estimation procedure. To illustrate this point, consider the system of estimating equations (97) and (98) above. Note that the terms $\Sigma_{m=1}^{M}\Sigma_{j=1}^{M}d_{mj}z_m^t z_j^t$ appear in each equation. The capital stock components $I_j^t, I_j^{t-1},\ldots,I_j^1$ appear as z_m^t's and there will be too many of these z_m^t's to estimate the parameters d_{mj} accurately. However, making use of the user cost approach, we may now add estimating equations of the form (99) for each component of the capital stock that has a user cost, where the w_i^t in (99) are replaced by the appropriate user cost $p_j^{t,\alpha}$ defined by (12). Alternatively, these investment goods may be taken out of the list of fixed capital stocks and can be put into the list of variable goods. Either way, we will dramatically increase the number of degrees of freedom available to estimate the parameters of technology. A second advantage of the user cost approach is that it allows us to avoid the restrictive a priori assumption of additive separability that is embodied in (114).

We conclude this section by noting an empirically useful special case for the user cost formula (120). In the absence of detailed empirical information on the period t market price for an investment good of class j that is α periods old, $Q_j^{t,\alpha}$, we may wish to assume that:

$$(121) \qquad Q_j^{t,\alpha} = (1-\delta_j)^{\alpha} Q_j^t .$$

where Q_j^t is the period t market price for one unit of a new investment good of class j and δ_j is the same average depreciation rate for investment goods of class j that was used in the previous section. A static expectations assumption that fits nicely with (121) is

$$(122) \qquad p_j^{t,\alpha} = (1-\delta_j)^{\alpha+1} Q_j^t \ .$$

Substitution of (121) and (122) into the user cost formula (120) yields

$$(123) \qquad p_j^{t,\alpha} = (1-\delta_j)^{\alpha}(1+r_t)^{-1}(r_t+\delta_j)Q_j^t \ .$$

Note that (123) is reasonably easy to implement empirically. The period t capital stock components for the firm are the vectors $k^0, I^1, I^2, \ldots, I^t$. With the jth component of these vectors, $k_j^0, I_j^1, I_j^1, \ldots, I_j^t$, we associate the corresponding period t user costs, $p_j^{t,t}, p_j^{t,t-1}, p_j^{t,t-2}, \ldots, p_j^{t,0}$, where these user costs could be defined by (120), or by (123) if we were willing to make the heroic assumptions (121) and (122).

8.6 Aggregation over Goods

Having constructed detailed price and quantity components for many outputs, many intermediate and labour inputs, and many variable components of the firm's capital stock, and having gathered detailed quantity information on the firm's fixed capital stock components and on its utilization of infrastructure services, the econometric investigator may be faced with the problem of having too much data to handle effectively. With the growth in the use of computers, many firms can now provide us with detailed price and quantity information on thousands of distinct goods. We will never be able to fit a second order approximation to a technology with a thousand goods, since this would require about 500,000 parameters. Hence, we will be forced to aggregate goods into a smaller number of aggregate commodities.

Needless to say, there is no known way of aggregating over goods that is completely unrestrictive. There are two main methods for justifying aggregating over goods in the context of producer theory. The first method was due to Hicks [1946;312-313] initially; see also Khang [1971] and Diewert [1978] [1980;434-438]. Hicks' Aggregation Theorem states that if the prices of a group of goods change in the same proportion, then that group of goods may be treated as if it were a single commodity. The problem with this result is that prices are unlikely to vary in an <u>exactly</u> proportional manner over time (or over producer units in the cross sectional context). The second major method for justifying aggregation over commodities is due to Shephard [1953;61-71][1970;145-146]. In this method, we assume that the firm's restricted profit function $\pi(p,s,k)$ has the following form:

$$(124) \qquad \pi(p_1,\ldots,p_K,p_{K+1},\ldots,p_N,s,k) = \hat{\pi}(f(p_1,\ldots,p_K),p_{K+1},\ldots,p_N,s,k)$$

where the function of K variables $c(p_1,\ldots,p_K)$ is linearly homogeneous. If x_n^t is the firm's net output of variable good n during period t and $p_n^t > 0$ is the corresponding price for $n = 1,2,\ldots,K$, then we may define an aggregate period t price for the first K variable goods P^t and a corresponding aggregate net output X^t by

$$(125) \qquad P^t \equiv c(p_1^t,\ldots,p_K^t) \quad ; \quad X^t \equiv (\Sigma_{n=1}^K p_n^t x_n^t)/P^t \quad ; \; t = 0,1,\ldots,T.$$

This second method for justifying the aggregation over goods is called the <u>homogeneous weak separability method</u>. Both methods are discussed in some detail with references to the literature in Diewert [1980;434-441].

Even if the homogeneous weak separability assumption (124) is true so that we can construct price and quantity aggregates by (125), we are still faced with a practical measurement problem: namely, what functional form should we pick for the function c in (125)?

Obviously it will be useful to pick a flexible functional form for c. Diewert [1976] shows that certain flexible functional forms for c are consistent with certain index number formulae such as Irving Fisher's [1922] ideal price and quantity index number formulae, which are the square roots of the products of the corresponding Paasche and Laspeyres price and quantity indexes. Similarly, if c has the translog functional form, then a certain index number formula for a price index (called the Törnqvist formula in Diewert [1976][1980;448], the Divisia price index in White [1985], and the translog price index in Jorgensen [1984b]) will generate <u>precisely</u> the P^t defined in (125). Moreover, we do not have to undertake any econometric estimation to construct the P^t via the use of an index number formula; all we require is price and quantity data for the K goods in the aggregate over the time periods under consideration. We will not go through the detailed mathematical derivations which justify the use of an index number formula to construct aggregates that are consistent with the homogeneous weak separability assumption (124); all the reader has to know is that the use of an INDEX statement in SHAZAM will construct price and quantity aggregates, P^t and X^t, which are consistent with (125) where c has the translog functional form. In more recent versions of SHAZAM, the Fisher ideal price and quantity indexes are also available.

We might also add that the use of the INDEX procedure in SHAZAM is also consistent with forming aggregates via Hicks' Aggregation Theorem; i.e., if the first K prices do happen to vary in proportion over time, the INDEX procedure will generate the theoretically correct price and quantity aggregates.

8.7 The Measurement of Infrastructure Variables

At this point, the reader should recall the 19 types of infrastructure services that we listed in section 1. In this subsection, we ask if there are any particular difficulties in measuring these variables.

The measurement difficulties appear to be fairly minimal with respect to the first 8 types of service listed under the utility and communication categories; we need only collect price and quantity data on the firm's utilization of these services in the normal way as outlined in section 8.1 above. For the most part, there will be user fees associated with each of these categories of service and we take these user fees to be our price variables. Irrigation services may also be treated in the same conventional manner.

However, the measurement difficulties are severe for the remaining categories of infrastructure services listed under the transportation and land development headings.

For example, consider the problem of measuring the stock of roads that is available to a given firm. Which roads are actually of some use to the firm? How can we aggregate the individual roads of varying quality (2 lane, 4 lane, paved, unpaved, etc.) into a small number of road stocks that will appear as s_i^t variables in our econometric model? We have no universally valid answers to these questions; the investigator will have to consider the data availability problems and experiment with alternative methods for aggregating the stocks of roads.

With the exception of irrigation projects, the classes of infrastructure services listed under land development projects do not seem to me to be suitable for the econometric approach (based on production theory) for mesuring the benefits of increases in infrastructure services. The problem is that the land development projects will tend to induce new firms to locate in the affected area and so measuring the increases in profits and rents of the pre project firms in the area will greatly underestimate the actual ex post benefits of a land development project. Thus a relatively crude approach which simply tried to measure the increase in land rents and profits of firms in the project affected area may be the best that we can do with respect to measuring the benefits of increases in infrastructure services in the land development categories.

Notes

For a general overview of data problems in the context of estimating econometric models, see Griliches [1984]. Other surveys of data problems are Diewert [1980] and Triplett [1983]. The vintage user cost approach to measuring capital outlined in section 8.5 has been suggested by Diewert [1980] and Mohr [1985].

For a survey of index number theory, see Diewert [1981b].

For a Hicks' Aggregation Theorem in the context of a dynamic model of producer behavior, see Epstein [1983]. See also Epstein [1981] for a discussion of functional form problems in dynamic production models.

9. The Estimation of Restricted Profit Functions in the Time Series Context

We turn now to a discussion of certain additional problems that occur if we are attempting to estimate a restricted profit function in the context of time series data.

The first problem we have to deal with is the existence of technical progress. Over time, firms will discover new ways for producing the same amount of output using smaller amounts of inputs. Our econometric model of the firm must take this fact into account. The simplest way to do this is to add time, t, as an explanatory variable. Thus instead of asking for a second order approximation to the restricted profit function $\pi(p,z)$, we now ask for such an approximation to $\pi(p,z,t)$.

Recall our old biquadratic restricted profit function defined by (93). We now add the following terms to the right hand side of (93):

$$(126) \qquad \Sigma_{n=1}^{N} a_{nt} t p_n^t + (\Sigma_{n=1}^{N} \gamma_n p_n^t)(\Sigma_{m=1}^{M} c_{mt} t z_m^t + (1/2) b_{tt} t^2)$$

where the N parameters a_{nt}, the M parameters c_{mt} and the one additional parameter b_{tt} must now be estimated along with the other parameters which appear in (93). The N nonnegative parameters γ_n should be determined in an a priori manner by the investigator, as were the β_n parameters. In fact, we may set $\gamma_n = \beta_n$ for $n = 1,\ldots,N$ but any nonnegative (but not identically zero) choices for the γ_n will preserve the second order approximation property of the biquadratic restricted profit function. With the additional terms defined by (126), we add the terms $a_{nt} t + \gamma_n(\Sigma_{m=1}^{M} c_{mt} t z_m^t + (1/2) b_{tt} t^2)$ to the right hand side of (98). If we are also using the ith inverse demand function for z_i, (99), in our system of estimating equations, then we add the term $(\Sigma_{n=1}^{N}\gamma_n p_n^t)c_{it}t$ to the right hand side of (99).

If we are working with the translog restricted profit function, we need to add the following terms to the right hand side of (86) in order to have a translog profit function that has the second order approximation property in the context of technical change:

$$(127) \qquad a_t t + \Sigma_{n=1}^{N} a_{nt} t \ell n p_n^t + \Sigma_{m=1}^{M} b_{mt} t \ell n z_m^t + (1/2)c_{tt}t^2$$

where the parameters a_{nt} must satisfy the restriction

$$(128) \qquad \Sigma_{n=1}^{N} a_{nt} = 0$$

in order to ensure that our new translog restricted profit function $\pi(p,z,t)$ is linearly homogeneous in the components of the price vector p. Note that taking into account (128), there are N + M + 1 additional independent parameters in (127), the same number of additional parameters as in (126). With the additional terms defined in (127), we must add the term $a_{nt}t$ to the right hand side of the nth share equation in our old estimating equation (92). If the firm is optimizing with respect to z_i and the user cost for z_i in period t is w_i^t, then our optimizing assumption implies $w_i^t = \partial\pi(p^t,z^t,t)/\partial z_i$ and upon differentiating our new translog restricted profit function and adding an error term ε_i^t, we may use the following estimating equations as well: for t = 1,2,...,T,

(129) $w_i^t z_i^t / p^t \cdot x^t = b_i + b_{it} t + \Sigma_{n=1}^N d_{ni} \ell n p_n^t + \Sigma_{j=1}^M e_{ij} \ell n z_j^t + \varepsilon_i^t$.

The above adjustments for dealing with technical change are very crude, but they are probably better than ignoring the problem altogether.

A second problem that can arise in the context of time series data is the aggregation over firms problem; i.e., the data that we have at our disposal may be industry or regional data, which gives us output and input aggregate or total data, rather than individual establishment data. In order to limit the length of this already overly long paper, we will not attempt to describe in detail the problems that can occur if we are forced to work with aggregate data instead of micro data pertaining to establishments. Suffice it to say that Hotelling [1935], May [1946] and Bliss [1975; 146] among others have noted that if all goods are variable and each production manager in each establishment is a price taking competitive profit maximizer, then the group of establishments or firms can be treated as if they were a single producer subject to the sum of the individual technology sets. This means we would have to put all of our infrastructure services variables s_i^f into the first class of N variable goods (this cannot be done if some $s_i^t = 0$ and there is no corresponding user cost price w_i^t) and we would have to put all of our "fixed" capital stocks k_j^f (except possibly one stock per firm that was truly fixed over the sample period) into the first class of variable goods as well (and thus we would require the existence of second hand markets for these capital goods). To sum up, working with aggregate data instead of firm or establishment micro data will create significant problems in implementing and interpreting our model of producer behaviour.

Notes

Our rather mechanical treatment of technological change follows that of Binswanger [1974]. More realistic theories of technical change with references to the literature are presented in Binswanger and Ruttan [1978], Griliches [1979], Denny, Everson, Fuss and Waverman [1981], Christensen, Cummings and Schoech [1983] and Kopp and Smith [1983]. In the last paper, the authors view technical change as arising through the adoption of process innovations involving new capital equipment. Thus in their view, much of the observed unexplained change in total factor productivity (i.e., technical change) can be explained by the necessarily imperfect aggregation of capital inputs that occurs in practice. For a brief survey of the "new goods problem," see Diewert [1980;498-505].

For analysis and references to the literature on the problems involved in aggregating over firms, see Gorman [1968], Diewert [1980;464-470], Fisher [1982] and Blackorby and Schworm [1982][1983a][1983b][1984].

10. The Estimation of Restricted Profit Functions in the Cross Sectional Context

The conceptual and measurement problems involved in empirically implementing our econometric models of producer behavior explained in section 7 above using just cross sectional data are very severe. We shall list some of the more important problems below.

(1) Often cross sectional data is industry data on outputs, inputs and the associated values and hence it suffers from the aggregation over firms problem mentioned in the previous section.

(2) Suppose that our cross sectional data consists of data on individual establishments producing a homogeneous product but the establishments are located in different countries or regions where relative prices are very, very different. Or suppose that our data comes from a single developed country, but that we wish to extrapolate our estimated technology to an underdeveloped country, where the price of labour might only be one per cent of the developed country's price of labour. Then the flexible functional forms for restricted profit functions defined in section 7 above may be totally inadequate to describe the industry's technology in such a global manner; i.e., when dealing with the large variations in relative prices that might occur when working with cross sectional data, a second order approximation to a technology set or the corresponding dual profit function may be totally inadequate.

(3) When we have time series data on a single establishment, firm or even industry, we may have some degree of confidence that our (aggregated) price and quantity data for outputs, intermediate inputs, labour and capital services has some degree of homogeneity; i.e., within each category, our aggregate output data say refers to roughly the same universe of disaggregated outputs. However, in dealing with cross sectional data, the individual establishments in our sample may be producing very different microeconomic outputs and using very different combinations of inputs. The highly aggregated data that we typically find in cross sectional samples may disguise the fact that the individual firms in our sample may well be producing totally different outputs and utilizing very different inputs. For example, the mix of labour services utilized in an industry in an underdeveloped country may be totally different from the mix utilized in the same industry in a developed country. What we are saying is that the aggregation over goods problem is

much more severe in the cross sectional context than in the time series context. This problem will tend to make our cross sectional econometric results virtually useless, unless a great deal of care is exercised.

(4) In the time series context, it is usually possible to find at least some crude price index deflators to deflate values into quantities. In the cross sectional context, it is virtually impossible to find the appropriate price deflators. If our cross sectional establishment data are taken from different regions within the same country, then it may be possible to find regional price indexes. However, typically, these regional indexes are not meant to be comparable across regions; i.e., they are constructed so that all regional prices equal 100 in the base year (and of course, all regional prices are not actually equal in the base year). There is a similar lack of comparability across units when we have an international cross section. Thus, when we have a cross sectional sample of data, we will require accurate information on values and quantities, whereas in the time series context, we can get by with just having information on values and price indexes.

(5) The measurement of capital stock components will be particularly difficult in the cross sectional context. We saw earlier in section 8.5 how the construction of accurate capital stock components required a great deal of time series information. This information will not be available if the investigator has only cross sectional data at his disposal. The use of historical book value of capital stock data will lead to enormous measurement errors, since there has been a great deal of inflation in developed countries in the last 40 years, and even more inflation in most underdeveloped countries.

In view of the above difficulties, we are not optimistic about the possibilities of accurately estimating technological parameters using cross sectional data.

However, if in spite of the above difficulties, the investigator wishes to proceed using only cross sectional data, we would recommend the use of the translog functional form rather than the biquadratic functional form. The reason for this choice is that we can make the translog parameter a_0 in (86) depend on the firm or establishment; i.e., replace a_0 by a_0^f when we fit the data for firm f. This will use up one degree of freedom per cross sectional unit, but this will not present a severe problem. In the biquadratic functional form, there does not appear to be a natural choice of a single parameter to be firm specific. This seems to be somewhat unfortunate, since as we have discussed above, we will not usually be able to impose the correct curvature conditions (recall the convexity in prices property for $\pi(p,z)$) globally on the translog functional form and maintain flexibility.

If the investigator can obtain data on the same establishments for at least two points in time (i.e., the investigator has <u>panel data</u> at his disposal), then the situation brightens up considerably. When working with the translog function form defined by (86) and (127), we can assume that a_0, a_n, $n = 1,\ldots,N$ and b_m, $m = 1,\ldots,M$ are firm specific but that the remaining parameters are constant across firms. When working with the biquadratic functional form defined by (93) and (126), we can assume that the N parameters a_n, $n = 1,\ldots,N$ and the M parameters d_{mm}, $m = 1,\ldots,M$ are firm specific while the remaining parameters are constant across firms.

This concludes our discussion of the econometric approach to estimating technology sets using restricted profit (or cost) functions.

Notes

We should remind the reader that we gained degrees of freedom for our econometric estimation by assuming price taking, profit maximizing behavior. Of course, this assumption of competitive behavior may not be satisfied in the real world. However, we can make crude adjustments to our procedure to take into account possible non competitive behavior; see Diewert [1974;155] [1982; 584-590], Lau [1974], Appelbaum [1979] and Appelbaum and Kohli [1979].

11. Conclusion

We have discussed a variety of approaches to measuring the benefits of investments in infrastructure services (or local public goods). Our simplest measure of benefits can be interpreted as the discounted increase in net outputs by producers in the project affected area less the discounted net cost of providing the extra infrastructure services, evaluated at constant (world) reference prices; see sections 2, 3 and 5.1. In section 5.2, we redefined our benefit measure to take into account the possible endogeneity of prices for some goods. In section 5.3, we further redefined our benefit measure to take into account possible benefits to consumers of the infrastructure investment project.

In sections 4 and 6.2, we developed an informationally parsimonious approach to the ex post measurement of infrastructure benefits in a static context. The approach required only price and quantity information for the pre and post project economies.

In section 6, we reviewed a number of alternative ex ante approaches to benefit measurement, including the questionnaire approach (section 6.1), the engineering approach (section 6.3), the applied general equilibrium modelling approach (section 6.4), and the differential approach (section 6.5). The econometric approach (section 6.6) yields valuable information on various elasticities of substitution (and on the second order derivatives of profit, cost and expenditure functions) and can be used as an input into the approaches explained in sections 6.3 to 6.5.

In view of the importance of the econometric approach, we devoted the rest of the paper (sections 7 through 10) to it.

Not one of the approaches to benefit measurement described in this paper is completely satisfactory; each of them suffers from one or more severe difficulties. However, each has some merit as well, so we leave the decision as to which method to use up to the reader. We hope that our discussion of the advantages and disadvantages of the various methods will be of some use to the reader.

Appendices 1 and 2 and sections 7 through 10 provide a fairly comprehensive overview of the functional form and data problems involved in the estimation of restricted profit and cost functions. Although much of our analysis can be found in the literature or is part of the oral tradition in the field, the present paper provides a convenient summary of many of the pitfalls. The biquadratic profit function defined by (93) is a new convenient functional form. Our suggested method for imposing globally valid curvature conditions consistent with flexibility is moderately new (actually, it is a straightforward adaptation of the method used by Diewert and Wales [1984] to impose the concavity in prices property on the Generalized McFadden cost function). Another "new" approach in this paper that may be of general interest is our suggested user cost treatment of capital; see (120) and (123).

We note two other results derived in this paper that may be of general interest.

The first result to be noted is the quadratic programming problem (76). This problem may be of interest not only to government infrastructure planners in market oriented economies, but also to central planners in socialist economies and to corporate planners in multiplant enterprises, who must allocate investment funds across industries or plants.

The second theoretical result that we wish to highlight is the idea of a "superlative" benefit measure (see (39) and (45)) that is exact for a certain theoretical benefit measure that is the average of certain profit <u>differences</u> of the form $\pi(p,s^1) - \pi(p,s^0)$ provided that π is a (flexible) biquadratic functional form. This is the counterpart to the superlative index number formula idea, where certain index number formula (such as the translog) are exact for certain theoretical indexes in the <u>ratio</u> form $\pi(p,s^1)/\pi(p,s^0)$ provided that π has a certain flexible functional form (such as the translog).

Appendix 1. Properties of Restricted Profit Functions

We assume that the production possibilities set T of a firm is a closed subset of N+M dimensional space. The first set of N goods corresponds to variable outputs and inputs; the second set of M goods corresponds to the firm's fixed capital stocks and to the amounts of infrastructure services that it is consuming. Thus if $(x,z)\varepsilon T$ [read: if the vectors $x \equiv (x_1,x_2,\ldots,x_N)$ and $z \equiv (z_1,z_2,\ldots,z_M)$ belong to the set T], then the firm has at its disposal the amounts $z_1,z_2,\ldots,z_M$ of the various types of capital and infrastructure services and it can produce (or utilize as an input if negative) amounts $x_1,x_2,\ldots,x_N$ of goods 1 to N respectively. We assume that the vector z is nonnegative (i.e. $z \geq 0_M$ where 0_M denotes a vector of zeros of dimension M), but the components of the vector x can be of either sign: if $x_1 > 0$, then the first good is being produced by the firm while if $x_1 < 0$, good 1 is being used as an input.

We assume that the firm faces positive prices $p \equiv (p_1,p_2,\ldots,p_N) \gg 0_N$ for its variable outputs and inputs. Given a nonnegative vector of fixed capital and infrastructure services $z \equiv \geq 0_M$, the firm will want to solve the following variable profit maximization problem:

$$(1) \qquad \max_x \{p\cdot x : (x,z)\varepsilon T\} \equiv \pi(p,z,T).$$

The objective function in the constrained maximization problem (1) is $p\cdot x \equiv \Sigma_{n=1}^N p_n x_n$ = revenues minus variable costs, since we have indexed inputs with a negative sign. The constraint in (1), $(x,z)\varepsilon T$, merely restricts the vector x to be technically feasible, given z. We have defined the optimized objective function in (1) to be the function π which depends on p (the vector of prices for variable goods that the firm faces), z (the firm's historically given vector of fixed capital and infrastructure services), and T (the firm's technology set). The function π is called the firm's restricted profit function. Other terms used for π in the literature include gross profit function; conditional profit function and the variable profit function.

Suppose that N=2 and M=1. Suppose further that the first variable good is an output and the second variable good is an input. Then the geometry of the firm's profit maximization problem (1) is illustrated in Figure 1 below.

Figure 1

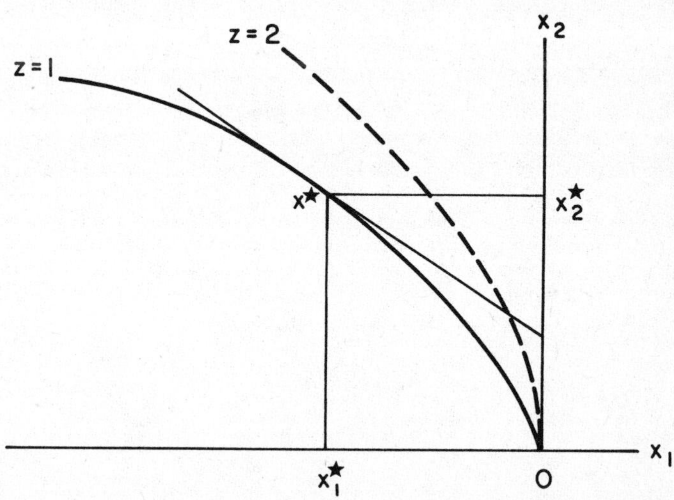

The set on or below the curved line is the set $\{(x_1,x_2) : (x_1,x_2,1)\varepsilon T\}$, the firm's production possibilites set for variable goods conditional on the fixed input level z=1. The point $x^* \equiv (x_1^*,x_2^*)$ solves the profit maximization problem (1) when z=1. The straight line passing through x* is the isoprofit line $\{(x_1,x_2) : p_1x_1+p_2x_2 = p_1x_1^*+p_2x_2^*\}$. This is the highest isoprofit line that still contains a technologically feasible x point. The point where this isoprofit line crosses the x_2 axis is $\pi(p,1,T)/p_2$. If z increases to z = 2, then the firm's production possibilities set for variable goods increases to the set on or below the dashed line. As p_1,p_2 and z change, the reader can use Figure 1 to determine how $\pi(p_1,p_2,z,T)$ changes.

As we shall be holding the technology set T constant throughout the analysis which follows, we shall drop the T argument in the π function.

We now consider what mathematical properties the function π might possess. Consider the following two properties:

Property 1: $\pi(p,z)$ is (positively) linearly homogeneous in the components of p for each fixed z. This means for $p \gg 0_N$, $z \geq 0_M$ and $\lambda > 0$, we have

$$(2) \qquad \pi(\lambda p,z) = \lambda\pi(p,z).$$

Property 2: $\pi(p,z)$ is a convex function of p for each fixed z. This means for every $z \geq 0_M$, $p^1 \gg 0_N$, $p^2 \gg 0_N$ and $0 \leq \lambda \leq 1$, we have

$$(3) \qquad \pi(\lambda p^1+(1-\lambda)p^2,z) \leq \lambda\pi(p^1,z) + (1-\lambda)\pi(p^2,z).$$

Proposition 1: Provided only that the relevant maxima exist, $\pi(p,z)$ defined by (1) has Properties 1 and 2 listed above.

Proof of Property 1: Let $p \gg 0_N$, $z \geq 0_M$ and $\lambda > 0$. Then

$$\pi(\lambda p,z) \equiv \max_x \{\lambda p\cdot x : (x,z)\varepsilon T\}$$
$$= \lambda \max_x \{p\cdot x : (x,z)\varepsilon T\} \qquad \text{since } \lambda \geq 0$$
$$\equiv \lambda\pi(p,z).$$

<u>Proof of Property 2</u>: Let $z \geq 0_M$, $p^1 \gg 0_N$, $p^2 \gg 0_N$ and $0 \leq \lambda \leq 1$. Then

$$\pi(\lambda p^1 + (1-\lambda)p^2,z) \equiv \max_x \{(\lambda p^1 + (1-\lambda)p^2)\cdot x : (x,z)\varepsilon T\}$$
$$= (\lambda p^1 + (1-\lambda)p^2)\cdot x^* \quad \text{say where } (x^*,z)\varepsilon T$$
$$= \lambda p^1\cdot x^* + (1-\lambda)p^2\cdot x^*$$
$$\leq \lambda \max_x \{p^1\cdot x : (x,z)\varepsilon T\} + (1-\lambda)p^2\cdot x^*$$

since x^* is feasible for the above maximization problem

$$\equiv \lambda\pi(p^1,z) + (1-\lambda)p^2\cdot x^*$$
$$\leq \lambda\pi(p^1,z) + (1-\lambda)\max_x \{p^2\cdot x : (x,z)\varepsilon T\}$$

since x^* is feasible for the above maximization problem

$$\equiv \lambda\pi(p^1,z) + (1-\lambda)\pi(p^2,z).$$

Q. E. D.

From the viewpoint of economics, Property 1 is straightforward: if all prices facing a competitive profit maximizing firm double, then profits will also double. However, Property 2 is not so straightforward. The property says that the profits a firm can get if it faces a weighted average $\lambda p^1 + (1-\lambda)p^2$ of two price vectors will generally be less than the same weighted average of the profits that it can get facing each price vector separately (the weights are λ and $(1-\lambda)$ in both cases). Figure 2 illustrates Property 2 in the N=2 case.

Figure 2

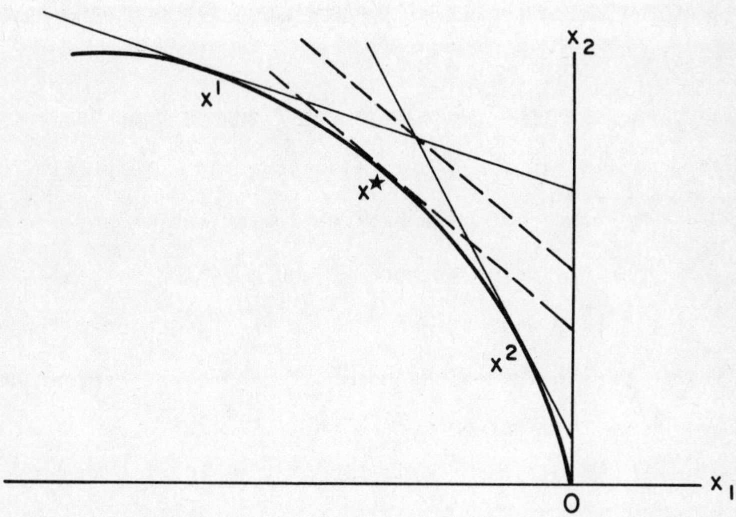

As was the case in Figure 1, we assume that good 1 is an input and good 2 is an output. The firm's production possibilities set for variable goods, $\{(x_1,x_2) : (x_1,x_2,z)\varepsilon T\}$, is the set on or below the curved line in Figure 2. When the price vector $p^1 \equiv (p_1^1,p_2^1)$ prevails, the firm maximizes profits at x^1; when prices $p^2 \equiv (p_1^2,p_2^2)$ prevail, the firm maximizes profits at x^2, and when the "average" prices $\lambda p^1 + (1-\lambda)p^2 \equiv (\lambda p_1^1 + (1-\lambda)p_1^2, \lambda p_2^1 + (1-\lambda)p_2^2)$ prevail, the firm maximizes profits at x^*. The lowest dashed isoprofit line represents the line $\{x : (\lambda p^1+(1-\lambda)p^2)\cdot x = (\lambda p^1+(1-\lambda)p^2)\cdot x^* = \pi(\lambda p^1+(1-\lambda)p^2,z)\}$ while the higher parallel dashed isoprofit line represents the line $\{x : (\lambda p^1+(1-\lambda)p^2)\cdot x = \lambda p^1\cdot x^1+(1-\lambda)p^2\cdot x^2 = \lambda\pi(p^1,z)+(1-\lambda)\pi(p^2,z)\}$, which passes through the intersection of the original two isoprofit lines. It can be seen that the inequality in (3) will be strict unless p^1 is proportional to p^2 or unless the technology set is "kinked" in such a way so that the point x^* is actually at the intersection of the original two isoprofit lines.

It is clear that the technology set T determines the functional form for the profit function $\pi(p,z)$. It is also true that the profit function may be used in order to construct an approximation to the technology set T. For example, consider the price vectors p^1 and p^2 which correspond to the points x^1 and x^2 in Figure 2 and define p^3 to be the "average" price vector $\lambda p^1 + (1-\lambda)p^2$ which corresponds to the point x^*. An outer approximation to the true technology set may be defined by the following set given that we know $\pi(p,z)$:

$$T(p^1,p^2,p^3) \equiv \{(x,z) : p^1 \cdot x \leq \pi(p^1,z);\ p^2 \cdot x \leq \pi(p^2,z) \text{ and } p^3 \cdot x \leq \pi(p^3,z),\ z \geq 0_M\}.$$

For the fixed z that corresponds to the curve in Figure 2, the above outer approximation to the true technology set yields the kinked set which lies below all three isoprofit lines through x^1, x^* and x^2. Note that this approximation is quite good in the sense that the kinked line is quite close to the curved line, at least for x_1 between x_1^1 and x_1^2. If we continue the above approximation process, taking additional positive price vectors p^i, then in the limit, we may define the best possible outer approximation to the true technology set T by

$$T^* \equiv \{(x,z) : p \cdot x \leq \pi(p,z) \text{ for every } p \gg 0\ ;\ z \geq 0\}. \tag{4}$$

If the original technology set is convex (i.e. $(x^1,z^1)\varepsilon T,(x^2,z^2)\varepsilon T, 0 \leq \lambda \leq 1$ implies $(\lambda x^1+(1-\lambda)x^2, \lambda z^1+(1-\lambda)z^2)\varepsilon T$ also), then the approximating set T* constructed using only the profit function π actually coincides with the original set T; i.e., there is a duality between convex production possibilities sets and profit functions in the sense that T and π provide completely equivalent characterizations of the technology.

Properties 1 and 2 for the profit function are very important. They are valid irrespective of the properties of the technology set. However, they do depend on the assumption of maximizing behaviour, which may not be true in empirical applications.

If we are willing to place some restrictions on the technology set T, we can derive additional properties that the profit function π will have.

A reasonable restriction to place on T is the property of free disposability of z goods. By this, we mean that T has the following property:

(5) $$0_M \leq z^1 \leq z^2,\ (x,z^1)\varepsilon T \text{ implies } (x,z^2)\varepsilon T.$$

Property (5) may be interpreted as follows: suppose that the vector of net outputs x is producible by the firm when it has available a certain vector z^1 of fixed capital stock components and infrastructure services. Then if more infrastructure services are made available to the firm, then x will still be producible.

Consider now the following property for π:

Property 3: $\pi(p,z)$ is a nondecreasing function of z for each fixed p. This means for $p \gg 0_N$, $0_M \leq z^1 \leq z^2$, we have

(6) $\pi(p,z^1) \leq \pi(p,z^2)$.

Proposition 2: If T satisfies the free disposability property (5), then π defined by (1) satisfies Property 3 above.

Proof: Let $p \gg 0_N$ and $0_M \leq z^1 \leq z^2$. Then

$$\begin{aligned}\pi(p,z^1) &\equiv \max_x \{p\cdot x : (x,z^1)\varepsilon T\} \\ &= p\cdot x^1 \quad \text{where } (x^1,z^1)\varepsilon T \\ &\leq \max_x \{p\cdot x : (x,z^2)\varepsilon T\}\end{aligned}$$

since by (5) $(x^1,z^2)\varepsilon T$ and hence x^1 is feasible for the maximization problem

$$\equiv \pi(p,z^2).$$

Q. E. D.

Another restriction which can be placed on the technology set T is the assumption of convexity, i.e., that T is a convex set. Unfortunately, this restriction is not innocuous, since it rules out any increasing returns to scale phenomena.

Consider the following property for π:

Property 4: $\pi(p,z)$ is a concave function of z for each fixed p. This means for each $p \gg 0$, $z^1 \geq 0$, $z^2 \geq 0_2$, $0 \leq \lambda \leq 1$, we have

(7) $\pi(p,\lambda z^1+(1-\lambda)z^2) \geq \lambda\pi(p,z^1)+(1-\lambda)\pi(p,z^2)$.

Proposition 3: If T is a convex set, then π defined by (1) satisfies Property 4 above.

Proof: Let $p \gg 0_N$, $z^1 \geq 0_M$, $z^2 \geq 0_M$ and $0 \leq \lambda \leq 1$. Let

(8) $$\pi(p,z^1) \equiv \max_x \{p \cdot x : (x,z^1) \varepsilon T\} = p \cdot x^1 \text{ so } (x^1,z^1) \varepsilon T \text{ and}$$

(9) $$\pi(p,z^2) \equiv \max_x \{p \cdot x : (x,z^2) \varepsilon T\} = p \cdot x^2 \text{ so } (x^2,z^2) \varepsilon T.$$

Since T is a convex set, $(\lambda x^1+(1-\lambda)x^2, \lambda z^1+(1-\lambda)z^2) \varepsilon T$. Thus

$$\begin{aligned}\pi(p,\lambda z^1+(1-\lambda)z^2) &\equiv \max_x \{p \cdot x : (x,\lambda z^1+(1-\lambda)z^2 \varepsilon T\} \\ &\geq p \cdot (\lambda x^1+(1-\lambda)x^2) \\ &\quad \text{since } \lambda x^1+(1-\lambda)x^2 \text{ is feasible for the maximization problem} \\ &= \lambda p \cdot x^1+(1-\lambda)p \cdot x^2 \\ &= \lambda \pi(p,z^1)+(1-\lambda)\pi(p,z^2) \\ &\quad \text{using (8) and (9).}\end{aligned}$$

Q. E. D.

Another restriction which can be placed on the technology set T is that the technology be subject to constant returns to scale, so that the set T is a cone; i.e., it satisfies the following property:

(10) $$(x,z) \varepsilon T, \ \lambda \geq 0 \text{ implies } (\lambda x, \lambda z) \varepsilon T.$$

The final property we wish to consider for π is:

Property 5: $\pi(p,z)$ is a (positively) linearly homogeneous function of z for each fixed p. This means for $p \gg 0_N$, $z \geq 0_M$ and $\lambda > 0$, we have

$$(11) \qquad \pi(p,\lambda z) = \lambda\pi(p,z).$$

Proposition 4: If T is a cone, then the corresponding profit function π defined by (1) has Property 5 above.

Proof: Let $p \gg 0_N$, $z \geq 0_M$ and $\lambda > 0$. Then

$$(12) \qquad \pi(p,z) \equiv \max_x \{p\cdot x : (x,z)\varepsilon T\} = p\cdot x^* \text{ say.}$$

$$\pi(p,\lambda z) \equiv \max_x \{p\cdot x : (x,\lambda z)\varepsilon T\}$$

$$(13) \qquad \geq p\cdot(\lambda x^*)$$

$$= \lambda\pi(p,z)$$

where the inequality follows from the feasibility of λx^* for the maximization problem. This feasibility follows from (12) which implies $(x^*,z)\varepsilon T$, and property (10) which implies $(\lambda x^*,\lambda z)\varepsilon T$. Now suppose the inequality in (13) were strict. This means there must exist $\tilde{x}$ such that $(\tilde{x},\lambda z)\varepsilon T$ and $p\cdot\tilde{x} > \lambda p\cdot x^*$ or since $\lambda > 0$,

$$(14) \qquad p\cdot(\tilde{x}/\lambda) > p\cdot x^* = \pi(p,z).$$

Since $(\tilde{x},\lambda z)\varepsilon T$, by (10), $(\tilde{x}/\lambda,z)\varepsilon T$ also. But now (14) contradicts (12). Thus our supposition is false, and the inequality (13) must be an equality. This establishes (11). Q. E. D.

If M=1, then we may plot $\pi(p,z)$ as a function of the scalar variable z. If T satisfies the free disposal property (5), then the curve $\pi(p,z)$ regarded as a function of z will have a nonnegative slope. If in addition, T is a convex set, the curve will be a concave function as in Figure 3. Finally, if in addition, T has the constant returns to scale property (10), the curve will be a straight line through the origin (see the dashed line in Figure 3).

Figure 3

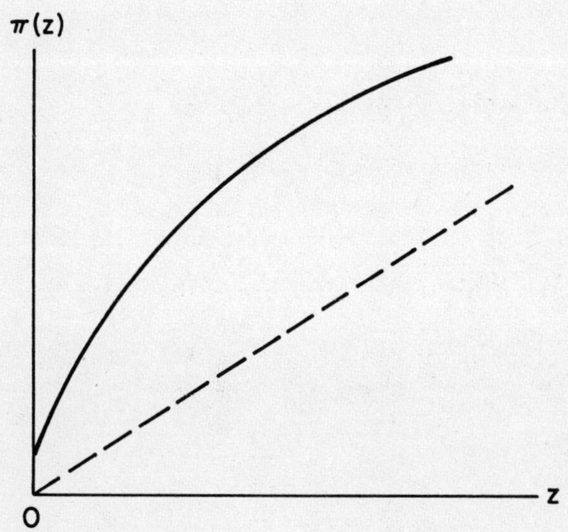

We now turn our attention to the properties of $\pi(p,z)$ assuming that it is differentiable with respect to its arguments. The following property is a fundamental one.

The Derivative Property of the Profit Function (Hotelling [1932;594]): Let T be given and define $\pi(p,z)$ by (1) above. In addition, suppose that π is once differentiable with respect to its N price arguments at the point $p^* \gg 0_N$, $z^* \underset{M}{\geq} 0$. Finally, let x^* denote a solution to the profit maximization problem $\max_x \{p^* \cdot x : (x,z^*) \varepsilon T\} \equiv \pi(p^*,z^*)$. Then x^* is the unique solution to the profit maximization problem and it is equal to the vector of first order partial derivatives of $\pi(p^*,z^*)$ with respect to the components of the price vector; i.e.,

$$(15) \qquad x^* = \nabla_p \pi(p^*,z^*).$$

The vector equation (15) is a brief way of writing the following N equations where $x^* \equiv (x_1^*, x_2^*, \ldots, x_N^*)$:

$$x_1^* = \partial\pi(p_1^*,\ldots,p_N^*,z_1^*,\ldots,z_M^*)/\partial p_1$$

$$x_2^* = \partial\pi(p_1^*,\ldots,p_N^*,z_1^*,\ldots z_M^*)/\partial p_2$$

$$\vdots$$

$$x_N^* = \partial\pi(p_1^*,\ldots,p_N^*,z_1^*,\ldots,z_M^*)/\partial p_N.$$

Proof: Since x^* solves the profit maximization problem when prices p^* prevail, we have

$$(16) \qquad \pi(p^*,z^*) = p^* \cdot x^*$$

with $(x^*,z^*) \varepsilon T$. Thus for any $p \gg 0_N$,

$$\pi(p,z^*) \equiv \max_x \{p \cdot x : (x,z) \varepsilon T\}$$

(17) $$\geq p \cdot x^*$$

since x* is feasible, but not necessarily optimal, for the maximization problem. Equality (16) and the inequalities (17) imply that the function of the N price variables $(p_1, p_2, \ldots, p_N) \equiv p$ defined by $g(p) \equiv \pi(p,z^*) - p \cdot x^*$ is nonnegative for all $p \gg 0_N$ but $g(p^*) = 0$. Thus g(p) attains a global minimum at $p = p^*$. Hence the following first order necessary conditions are satisfied:

(18) $$\nabla_p g(p^*) = \nabla_p \pi(p^*,z^*) - x^* = 0_N.$$

(18) may be rearranged to yield (15). Q. E. D.

The inequality (17) which is the key to the above derivative property is illustrated in Figure 4.

Figure 4

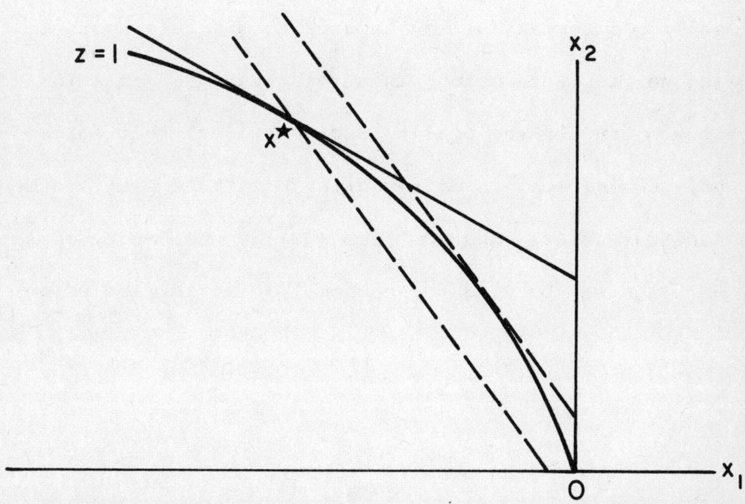

The curved line in Figure 4 corresponds to the curved line in Figure 1; each point on the curve gives the maximum amount of output x_2 that can be produced given an amount of variable input equal to $-x_1$ and given an amount of fixed input $z = 1$ (essentially, the curve is the firm's short run production function). The isoprofit line tangent to the curve at the point x^* corresponds to the line $\{x : p^* \cdot x = p^* \cdot x^*\}$. The dashed line through x^* corresponds to the line $\{x : p \cdot x = p \cdot x^*\}$. The higher parallel dashed line corresponds to the highest isoprofit line that is feasible when the producer faces prices p, which is the line $\{x : p \cdot x = \pi(p,z^*)\}$. Since the second line is higher, we have $\pi(p,z^*) \geq p \cdot x^*$ which is (17).

Thus, if $\pi(p,z)$ is differentiable with respect to the components $p_1,\ldots,p_N$ of the price vector p for outputs and variable inputs, the firm's nth profit maximizing <u>net supply function</u> (this is minus a demand function if good n is used as an input) $x_n(p,z)$ can be obtained by partially differentiating $\pi(p,z)$ with respect to p_n; i.e., we have

$$(19) \qquad x_n(p,z) = \partial\pi(p,z)/\partial p_n \qquad n = 1,\ldots,N.$$

Hotelling's Lemma (19) may be used to generate systems of profit maximizing net suply functions in a relatively easy fashion: simply postulate a functional form for the profit function $\pi(p,z)$ that satisfies Properties 1 and 2 and, in addition, is differentiable with respect to the components of p. Then differentiate, and equation (19) is the desired system of net supply functions which may be used for econometric estimation purposes. In order to avoid an expensive nonlinear regression problem, it will be necessary to choose the functional form for $\pi(p,z)$ in such a way so that the price derivatives $\partial\pi(p,z)/\partial p_n$ (or a transformation of them) are linear in the unknown parameters which characterize the functional form for π.

If $f(x)$ is a linearly homogeneous differentiable function, (i.e., $f(\lambda x) = \lambda f(x)$ for all $\lambda > 0$ and $x \gg 0_N$), then Euler's Theorem on homogeneous functions implies the following identity:

$$(20) \qquad f(x) = x \cdot \nabla f(x) \equiv \Sigma_{n=1}^{N} x_n \partial f(x_1,\ldots,x_N)/\partial x_n.$$

(To prove (20), differentiate both sides of $f(\lambda x) = \lambda f(x)$ with respect to λ and set $\lambda = 1$.)

If our linearly homogeneous f happens to be twice continuously differentiable with respect to its arguments (this means that each second order partial derivative function $\partial^2 f(x_1,\ldots,x_N)/\partial x_i \partial x_j$ exists and is a continuous function of its arguments), then we can derive further restrictions on the derivatives of f that must hold. Partially differentiate both sides of the equation $f(\lambda x) = \lambda f(x)$ with respect to x_i. We obtain the equation $\lambda \partial f(\lambda x)/\partial x_i = \lambda \partial f(x)/\partial x_i$ or $\partial f(\lambda x)/\partial x_i = \partial f(x)/\partial x_i$. Now differentiate this last equation with respect to λ and set $\lambda = 1$. We obtain the following equation:

$$(21) \qquad \Sigma_{j=1}^{N} [\partial^2 f(x_1,\ldots,x_N)/\partial x_i \partial x_j] x_j = 0.$$

Since the index i could be any integer between 1 and N, (21) holds for i = 1,2,...,N. The resulting N equations can be expressed more succinctly as follows:

$$\text{(22)} \qquad \nabla^2 f(x)x = 0_N$$

where $\nabla^2 f(x) \equiv \begin{bmatrix} \partial^2 f(x)/\partial x_1 \partial x_1, \ldots, \partial^2 f(x)/\partial x_1 \partial x_N \\ \vdots \qquad\qquad\qquad \vdots \\ \partial^2 f(x)/\partial x_N \partial x_1, \ldots, \partial^2 f(x)/\partial x_N \partial x_N \end{bmatrix}$

is the N by N matrix of second order partial derivatives of f.

A final set of restrictions on the derivatives of f is implied by our assumption that f is twice continuously differentiable. Under these conditions, Young's Theorem implies that the order in which we differentiate to form the second order partial derivatives is immaterial; i.e., we have

$$\text{(23)} \qquad \partial^2 f(x_1,\ldots,x_N)/\partial x_i \partial x_j = \partial^2 f(x_1,\ldots,x_N)/\partial x_j \partial x_j \quad \text{for all } i \neq j.$$

The N(N-1)/2 symmetry relations can be expressed more succinctly using matrix notation; i.e., we have

$$\text{(24)} \qquad [\nabla^2 f(x)]^T = \nabla^2 f(x)$$

so that the Hessian matrix of second order partial derivatives, $\nabla^2 f(x)$, is symmetric (A^T denotes the transpose of the matrix A).

The above digression on the properties of linearly homogeneous functions has an application to the profit function $\pi(p,z)$ since it is linearly homogeneous in p.

Thus, if $\pi(p,z)$ is once differentiable with respect to its p components, using Hotelling's Lemma (19) and Euler's Theorem (20), we deduce the following equalities:

$$(25) \qquad \pi(p,z) = \Sigma_{n=1}^{N} p_n \partial\pi(p,z)/\partial p_n = \Sigma_{n=1}^{N} p_n x_n(p,z),$$

where the $x_n(p,z)$ are the profit maximizing net supply functions discussed earlier.

Equation (25) has an important econometric implication: the profit function $\pi(p,z)$ does not contain any additional information that is not already contained in the net supply functions $x_n(p,z)$. Thus if all N of the net supply functions $x_n(p,z)$ are estimated econometrically, the profit function equation should not be appended to the estimating equations.

If $\pi(p,z)$ is twice continuously differentiable with respect to the components of the p vector, then we may utilize (22) and (24) and derive some interesting results. Let us form the N by N matrix of derivatives of the net supply functions $x_n(p,z)$ defined by (19):

$$\nabla_p x(p,z) \equiv \begin{bmatrix} \partial x_1(p,z)/\partial p_1,\ldots,\partial x_1(p,z)/\partial p_N \\ \vdots \\ \partial x_N(p,z)/\partial p_1,\ldots,\partial x_N(p,z)/\partial p_N \end{bmatrix}$$

$$= \begin{bmatrix} \partial^2\pi(p,z)/\partial p_1\partial p_1,\ldots,\partial^2\pi(p,z)/\partial p_1\partial p_N \\ \vdots \\ \partial^2\pi(p,z)/\partial p_N\partial p_1,\ldots,\partial^2\pi(p,z)/\partial p_N\partial p_N \end{bmatrix} \quad \text{using (19)}$$

(26) $$\equiv \nabla^2_{pp}\pi(p,z).$$

The matrix equation (26) says that the matrix of price derivatives of the N net supply functions $x(p,z)$ is equal to the N by N matrix of second order partial derivatives of the profit function $\pi(p,z)$ with respect to its price arguments. The symmetry restrictions (24) imply that these price derivatives cannot be independent; i.e., we have $\partial x_i(p,z)/\partial p_j = \partial x_j(p,z)/\partial p_i$ for all $i \neq j$. In matrix notation, these restrictions may be written as

(27) $$[\nabla_p x(p,z)]^T = [\nabla_p x(p,z)].$$

This matrix of price derivatives also satisfies the following counterpart to the adding up restrictions (22):

(28) $$[\nabla_p x(p,z)]p = 0_N.$$

Recall Property 2 for π; i.e., that $\pi(p,z)$ be a convex function of p for each fixed z. If $\pi(p,z)$ is twice continuously differentiable with respect to the components of p, then it can be shown (e.g., see Fenchel [1953;87-88],

Rockafellar [1970;27] or Varian [1978;253]) that $\nabla^2_{pp}\pi(p,z)$ must be a positive semidefinite symmetric matrix. (An N by N symmetric matrix A is positive definite if $x^TAx > 0$ for all $x \neq 0_N$ and is positive semidefinite if $x^TAx \geq 0$ for all $x \neq 0_N$). Thus we have our final set of restrictions on the price derivatives of the net supply functions:

(29) $$[\nabla_p x(p,z)] = \nabla^2_{pp}\pi(p,z) \text{ is a positive semidefinite matrix.}$$

Using the definition of positive semidefiniteness, it can be verified that (29) implies the following N inequalities:

(30) $$\partial x_n(p,z)/\partial p_n = \partial^2\pi(p,z)/\partial p_n\partial p_n \geq 0, \qquad n = 1,\ldots N.$$

The equalities (30) tell us that the profit maximizing net supply function for good n cannot slope downwards. If good n is an output, then $x_n(p,z)$ is positive and an increase in p_n will increase (or at least not decrease) the supply of that good. If good n is an input, then $x_n(p,z)$ is negative and an increase in p_n will make this negative demand for good n less negative, i.e., the demand for good n will decrease (or at least not increase). Thus the inequalities (30) tell us that the firm's supply functions will slope upwards and their input demand functions will slope downwards.

Note that we have derived the core of the microeconomic theory of the firm in a relatively simple manner, without having to invert a single matrix. For a more traditional approach, see Hicks [1946;319-323].

The restrictions (29) have econometric implications as well. After one has estimated econometrically the unknown parameters which characterize

$\pi(p,z)$, one must check whether the positive semidefiniteness restrictions (29) are satisfied at each sample point. Alternatively, we require a method for imposing these restrictions.

We now turn our attention to the properties of $\pi(p,z)$ when π is differentiable with respect to the components of $z \equiv (z_1,\ldots,z_M)$. Clearly, from the definition of a derivative, the partial derivative of $\pi(p,z)$ with respect to z_m is the rate of increase in net revenue from the production of variable goods with respect to the mth fixed capital stock, holding constant the other capital stocks. In economics terminology, $\partial\pi(p,z)/\partial z_m \equiv w_m(p,z)$ is the marginal change in profits due to the addition of a marginal unit of z_m. A profit maximizing firm should be willing to pay this price w_m for the use of the extra marginal unit of z_m, so we call $w_m(p,z)$ the mth <u>willingness to pay function</u>. We may form a vector of these willingness to pay functions by partially differentiating $\pi(p,z)$ with respect to the components of z:

$$(31)\qquad w(p,z) \equiv \begin{bmatrix} w_1(p,z) \\ \vdots \\ w_M(p,z) \end{bmatrix} \equiv \begin{bmatrix} \partial\pi(p,z)/\partial z_1 \\ \vdots \\ \partial\pi(p,z)/\partial z_M \end{bmatrix} \equiv \nabla_z \pi(p,z).$$

If the production possibilities set T satisfies the free disposal property (5), then the willingness to pay functions are nonnegative, i.e., $w(p,z) \geq 0_M$.

If the set T is convex, then by Proposition 3, $\pi(p,z)$ is a concave function of z for each fixed p. If in addition, $\pi(p,z)$ is twice continuously differentiable with respect to its z arguments, then the Hessian matrix of second order partial derivatives of π with respect to its z arguments, $\nabla^2_{zz}\pi(p,z)$, must be a negative semidefinite symmetric M by M matrix. Now form the M by M matrix of derivatives of the M willingness to pay functions w(p,z) with respect to the components of z:

$$\nabla_z w(p,z) \equiv \begin{bmatrix} \partial w_1(p,z)/\partial z_1, \ldots, \partial w_1(p,z)/\partial z_M \\ \vdots \qquad\qquad \vdots \\ \partial w_M(p,z)/\partial z_1, \ldots, \partial w_M(p,z)/\partial z_M \end{bmatrix}$$

$$= \begin{bmatrix} \partial^2\pi(p,z)/\partial z_1\partial z_1, \ldots, \partial^2\pi(p,z)/\partial z_1\partial z_M \\ \vdots \qquad\qquad \vdots \\ \partial^2\pi(p,z)/\partial z_M\partial z_1, \ldots, \partial^2\pi(p,z)/\partial z_M\partial z_M \end{bmatrix} \quad \text{using (31)}$$

$$(32) \qquad \equiv \nabla^2_{zz}\pi(p,z).$$

Equation (32) says that the matrix of quantity derivatives of the M willingness to pay functions w(p,z) is equal to the M by M matrix of second order partial derivatives of the profit function $\pi(p,z)$ with respect to the components of the infrastructure services and fixed capital vector $z \equiv (z_1,\ldots,z_M)$. The symmetry restrictions (24) applied to our present model that these quantity derivatives cannot be independent; i.e., we have $\partial w_i(p,z)/\partial z_j = \partial w_j(p,z)/\partial z_i$ for all $i \neq j$. In matrix notation, these restrictions may be written as

$$(33) \qquad [\nabla_z w(p,z)]^T = [\nabla_z w(p,z)].$$

Recall that the concavity of $\pi(p,z)$ in z implies that its Hessian matrix with respect to the components of z is negative semidefinite. In this case, we have

$$(34) \qquad \nabla_z w(p,z) = \nabla^2_{zz}\pi(p,z) \text{ is a negative semidefinite matrix.}$$

The matrix $\nabla^2_{zz}\pi(p,z)$ is negative semidefinite if and only if $y^T[\nabla^2_{zz}\pi(p,z)]y \leq 0$ for all $y \neq 0_M$. Thus (34) implies the following M inequalities:

$$(35) \qquad \partial w_m(p,z)/\partial z_m = \partial^2\pi(p,z)/\partial z_m\partial z_m \leq 0, \qquad m = 1,\ldots,M.$$

The inequalities (35) tell us that the willingness to pay functions are downward sloping (at least not upward sloping), provided that the technology set T is assumed to be convex.

Let us assume that M=1 and T is a convex set that has the free disposal property (5). The the graphs of $\pi(p,z)$ and $w(z) \equiv \partial\pi(p,z)/\partial z$ might look like the curves graphed in Figure 5.

Figure 5

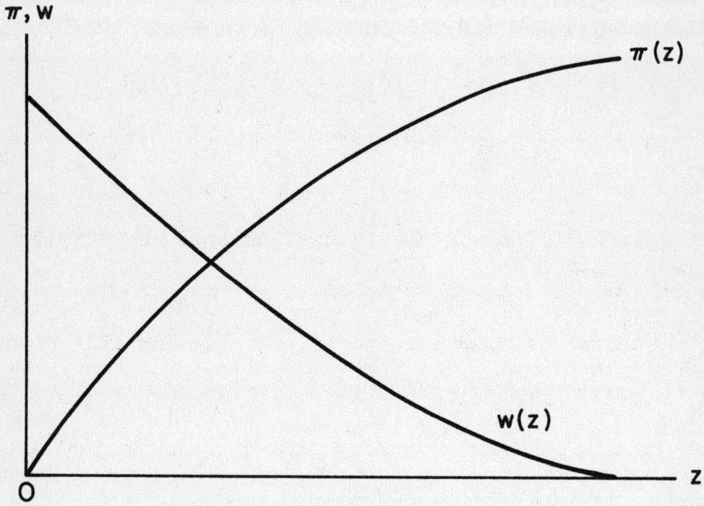

If $\pi(p,z)$ is twice continuously differentiable with respect to both sets of arguments, we may apply Young's Theorem 24 and conclude that the derivative of the mth willingness to pay function in (31) with respect to the nth price p_n, $\partial w_m(p,z)/\partial p_n$, is equal to the derivative of the nth net supply function in (15) with respect to the mth quantity z_m, $\partial x_n(p,z)/\partial z_m$; i.e., we have for all $n=1,2,\ldots,N$ and all $m=1,2,\ldots M$

(36) $$\partial w_m(p,z)/\partial p_n = \partial^2\pi(p,z)/\partial z_m\partial p_n = \partial^2\pi(p,z)/\partial p_n\partial z_m = \partial x_n(p,w)/\partial z_m.$$

Finally, suppose that T is a cone so that by Proposition 4, $\pi(p,z)$ is linearly homogeneous in z. Assuming also that π is twice continuously differentiable with respect to its arguments leads to the following restrictions on the derivatives of π:

(37) $$\pi(p,z) = \Sigma_{m=1}^{M} z_m \partial\pi(p,z)\partial z_m = \Sigma_{m=1}^{M} z_m w_m(p,z);$$

(38) $$[\nabla_{zz}^2 \pi(p,z)]z = 0_M \quad ;$$

(39) $$[\nabla_{pz}^2 \pi(p,z)]z = \nabla_p \pi(p,z) = x(p,z).$$

(37) follows from (20) upon identifying z as an x and (38) follows from (22). Equations (39) may be derived as follows. We have the equation $\pi(p,\lambda z) = \lambda\pi(p,z)$. Partially differentiate this last equation with respect to p_n and obtain the equation $\partial\pi(p,\lambda z)/\partial p_n = \lambda\partial\pi(p,z)/\partial p_n$. Thus the function $\partial\pi(p,z)/\partial p_n$ is linearly homogeneous in z and we may apply (20) to this function to get the following equation:

(40) $$\Sigma_{m=1}^{M} [\partial^2\pi)p,z)/\partial p_n \partial z_m] z_m = \partial\pi(p,z)/\partial p .$$

Equation (40) is the nth equation in (39). Repeating (40) for n=1,2,...,N yields (39).

Using the fact that $\pi(p,z)$ is linearly homogeneous in the components of p, we can deduce the following counterpart to (39) where the roles of p and z have been interchanged:

(41) $$[\nabla_{zp}^2 \pi(p,z)]p = \nabla_z \pi(p,z) = w(p,z).$$

These restrictions on the derivatives of π play a role in determining whether a given functional form can approximate an arbitrary function to the second order.

Notes

Complete duality theorems between production possibilities sets T and restricted profit functions may be found in Gorman [1968], McFadden [1978] and Diewert [1973]. The symmetry restrictions (27) and the positive semidefiniteness conditions (29) were first obtained by Hotelling [1932;594] [1935;69-70]. The reciprocity relations (36) were first obtained by Samuelson [1953-4] in a somewhat simpler model. The complete set of restrictions that we have developed in this Appendix were obtained by Diewert [1974;142-146]. Additional references to the literature may be found in Diewert [1982;583-4]. The method of proof used to establish the derivative property for profit functions, (15), was used by Karlin [1959;272].

Appendix 2. Properties of Restricted Cost Functions

We assume that the production possibilities set of the government T is a closed subset of N+I+J dimensional space. The first set of N goods corresponds to amounts of variable inputs used by the government, the second set of I goods corresponds to government infrastructure services that the government is producing and the third set of J goods corresponds to amounts of fixed capital services that the government has at its disposal. Thus if $(x,s,k)\varepsilon T$, then the government has at its disposal the amounts $(x_1,x_2,\ldots,x_N) \equiv x$ of the n types of variable input and amounts $(k_1,k_2,\ldots,k_J) \equiv k$ of the J types of capital input services and can produce the amounts $(s_1,s_2,\ldots,s_I)$ of the various types of infrastructure services. We assume that $x \geq 0_N$, $s \geq 0_I$ and $k > 0_J$ so that all goods are measured as nonnegative quantities. (Note that we have reversed our sign convention on x goods made in Appendix 1).

We assume that the government faces positive prices $p \equiv (p_1, p_2, \ldots p_N) \gg 0_N$ for its variable inputs. Given that the government has at its disposal the vector $k \geq 0_J$ of fixed capital stocks and that it wishes to produce the vector $s \geq 0_I$ of government infrastructure services, an efficient government will want to solve the following cost minimization problem:

$$(1) \qquad \min_x \{p \cdot x : (x,s,k) \in T\} \equiv c(p,s,k).$$

If the components of the vector of service targets s are so large relative to the vector of capital stocks k that the government has on hand, then there may be no feasible x vector such that (x,s,k) belongs to T. In this case, we define the minimized objective function for the constrained minimization problem (1), c(p,s,k), to be $+\infty$.

The minimized objective function for the constrained minimization problem (1) may be regarded as a function of p, s and k. This function, c(p,s,k), is called the government's restricted cost function. This function also depends on the technology set T, but since we will be holding the technology set constant in this Appendix, we have written c(p,s,k,T) as c(p,s,k).

Suppose that there are two variable inputs (i.e., N=2), one government service (i.e., I=1) and one government capital stock (i.e., J=1). Then the geometry of the government's cost minimization problem (1) can be illustrated by Figure 1 below.

Figure 1.

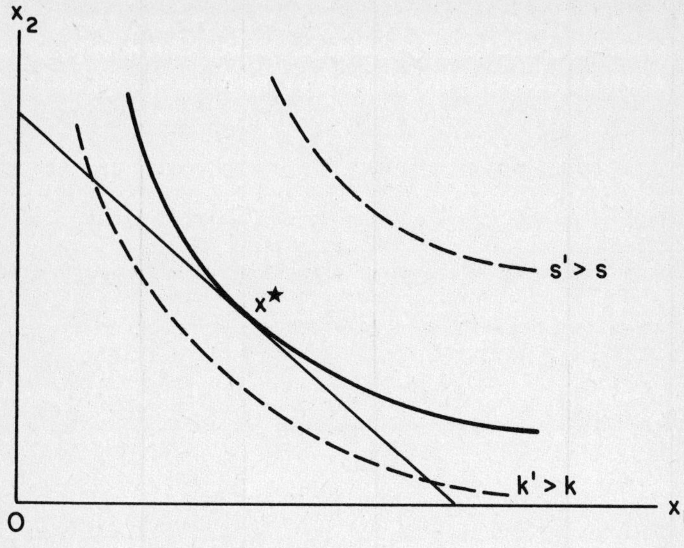

The solid curved line in Figure 1 is the lower boundary of the set $\{(x_1,x_2) : (x_1,x_2,s,k)\varepsilon T\}$, the set of variable input combinations that can produce the output s given that the government has the fixed capital stock k at its disposal. The point $x^* \equiv (x_1^*,x_2^*)$ solves the cost minimization problem (1). The straight line passing through x* is the isocost line $\{(x_1,x_2) : p_1x_1 + p_2x_2 = p_1x_1^* + p_2x^*_2\}$. This is the lowest isocost line that still contains a technologically feasible x point. The point where this isocost line crosses the x_2 axis is $c(p,s,k)/p_2$. If the government's output target is increased to s' > s, the curved line will generally shift upwards, say to the dashed line labelled s' > s. In this mental experiment, the capital stock k is held fixed. On the other hand, if the output target remains at s but the capital stock increases to k', the curved line will generally shift downwards.

Consider the following two properties for c:

Property 1: c(p,s,k) is (positively) linearly homogeneous in the components of p for each fixed s,k such that c(p,s,k) is finite for some p; i.e., for $p \gg 0_N$, $s \geq 0_I$, $k \geq 0_J$, $\lambda > 0$ and c(p,s,k) finite we have

$$(2) \qquad c(\lambda p,s,k) = \lambda c(p,s,k).$$

Property 2: c(p,s,k) is a concave function of p for each fixed s,k such that c(p,s,k) is finite for some p; i.e., for $p^1 \gg 0_N$, $p^2 \gg 0_N$, $0 \leq \lambda \leq 0$, $s \geq 0_I$, $k \geq 0_J$, we have

$$(3) \qquad c(\lambda p^1+(1-\lambda)p^2,s,k) \geq \lambda c(p^1,s,k) + (1-\lambda)c(p^2,s,k).$$

Proposition 1: Provided only that the relevant minima exist, the restricted cost function c(p,s,k) defined by (1) has Properties 1 and 2 listed above.

The proof of this Proposition is an exact analogue to the Proof of Proposition 1 in Appendix 1, except minima replace maxima and thus the various inequalities are reversed. Thus c(p,s,k) has a concavity property in prices whereas $\pi(p,z)$ had a convexity property in prices.

Recall that the restricted profit function $\pi(p,z)$ could be used to form an outer approximation T* to the true technology set T, an approximation which was exact if the original technology set T was convex. A similar duality theorem holds for the restricted cost function. The outer approximation to the true technology set is now defined by

(4) $T^* \equiv \{(x,s,k) : p \cdot x \geq c(p,s,k) \text{ for every } p \gg 0_N;\ s \geq 0_J;\ k \geq 0_J\}.$

If the original technology set T is convex, then the approximating set T* will coincide with the original set T.

If we place restrictions on the underlying government technology set T, then we may show that the restricted cost function c defined by (1) satisfies properties in addition to the linear homogeneity and concavity in prices properties, Properties 1 and 2 listed above.

We say that T satisfies a free disposal property in outputs and fixed inputs if and only if the following condition is true:

(5) $0_J \leq k^1 \leq k^2,\ 0_I \leq s^2 \leq s^1,\ (x,s^1,k^1) \varepsilon T \text{ implies } (x,s^2,k^2) \varepsilon T.$

Thus if a certain output vector s^1 is producible by the variable input vector x and the fixed input vector k^1, s^2 is a lesser output vector and k^2 is a greater fixed input vector, then x and k^2 can produce s^2.

Property 3: c(p,s,k) is nondecreasing in the components of s and nonincreasing in the components of k for fixed p; i.e., for $p \gg 0_N$, $s \geq 0_I$, $k \geq 0_J$, c(p,s,k) finite, then

(6) $0_I \leq s' \leq s$ implies $c(p,s',k) \leq c(p,s,k)$ and

(7) $0_J \leq k \leq k'$ implies $c(p,s,k) \geq c(p,s,k')$.

Proposition 2: If T satisfies (5), then c defined by (1) satisfies Property 3 above.

<u>Proof</u>: Let $p \gg 0_N$, $s \geq 0_I$, $k \geq 0_J$, $c(p,s,k)$ be finite, $0_I \leq s' \leq s$, and $k \leq k'$. Then

$$
\begin{aligned}
c(p,s,k) &\equiv \min_x \{p \cdot x : (x,s,k) \in T\} \\
&= p \cdot x^* \quad \text{where } (x^*,s,k) \in T \\
&\geq \min_x \{p \cdot x : (x,s',k) \in T\} \qquad (8) \\
&\equiv c(p,s',k)
\end{aligned}
$$

which establishes (6). The inequality (8) follows from the feasibility of (x^*,s,k) for the minization problem. This feasibility follows from $(x^*,s,k) \in T$, $0 \leq s' \leq s$ and property (5), where we let $k^1 = k^2 \equiv k$, $s^2 \equiv s'$, $s^1 \equiv s$ and $x \equiv x^*$. We also have

$$
\begin{aligned}
c(p,s,k) &\equiv \min_x \{p \cdot x : (x,s,k) \in T\} \\
&= p \cdot x^* \quad \text{where } (x^*,s,k) \in T \\
&\geq \min_x \{p \cdot x : (x,s,k') \in T\} \\
&\equiv c(p,s,k')
\end{aligned}
$$

where the inequality follows from the feasibility of (x^*,s,k) for the minimization problem and the feasibility follows from (5) letting $k^1 \equiv k$, $k^2 \equiv k'$, $s^1 = s^2 \equiv s$ and $x \equiv x^*$. Q. E. D.

Another possibile property for c is:

<u>Property 4</u>: c(p,s,k) is a convex function in the components of s,k for each fixed p; i.e., for $p \gg 0_N$, $s^1 \geq 0_I$, $s^2 \geq 0_I$, $k^1 \geq 0_J$, $k^2 \geq 0_J$, $0 \leq \lambda \leq 1$, $c(p,\lambda s^1+(1-\lambda)s^2,\lambda k^1+(1-\lambda)k^2)$ finite, we have

$$c(p,\lambda s^1+(1-\lambda)s^2,\lambda k^1+(1-\lambda)k^2 \leq \lambda c(p,s^1,k^1) + (1-\lambda)c(p,s^2,k^2). \tag{9}$$

<u>Proposition 3</u>: If T is a convex set, then c defined by (1) satisfies Property 4 above.

The proof is an analogue to the proof of Proposition 3 in Appendix 1, where a minimum replaces a maximum and hence the inequality is reversed.

A final restriction which can be placed on the technology set T is that the technology be subject to constant returns to scale, so that T is a cone; i.e., we have

$$(x,s,k)\varepsilon T,\ \lambda \geq 0 \text{ implies } (\lambda x,\lambda s,\lambda k)\varepsilon T. \tag{10}$$

The final property we wish to consider for π is:

<u>Property 5</u>: c(p,s,k) is a (positively) linearly homogeneous function of s and k for each fixed p; i.e. for $p \gg 0_N$, $s \geq 0_I$, $k \geq 0_J$, $\lambda > 0$, c(p,s,k) finite,

$$c(p,\lambda s,\lambda k) = \lambda c(p,x,k). \tag{11}$$

<u>Proposition 4</u>: If T is a cone, then the corresponding restricted cost function c defined by (1) has Property 5.

The proof of Proposition 4 is exactly analogous to the proof of Proposition 4 in Appendix 1.

Let us consider the geometric significance of Properties 4 and 5. Suppose N and J are arbitrary and I=1 so that the government is producing only one service. We wish to study the variation of variable cost, c(p,s,k) as a function of the scalar service variable s. If T satisfies the free disposal property 5, then c(p,s,k) is nondecreasing in s. If in addition, the technology set T is convex, then the graph of c as a function of s will have the general slope depicted by Figure 2. The derivative of c with respect to s, $\partial c(p,s,k)/\partial s \equiv m(p,s,k)$, is the marginal cost function and it is depicted by the dashed curve. If T were a cone and J=0, then the cost curve would become a straight line passing through the origin with a positive slope, and the marginal cost curve would be a constant function equal to the constant slope of the cost curve.

Figure 2

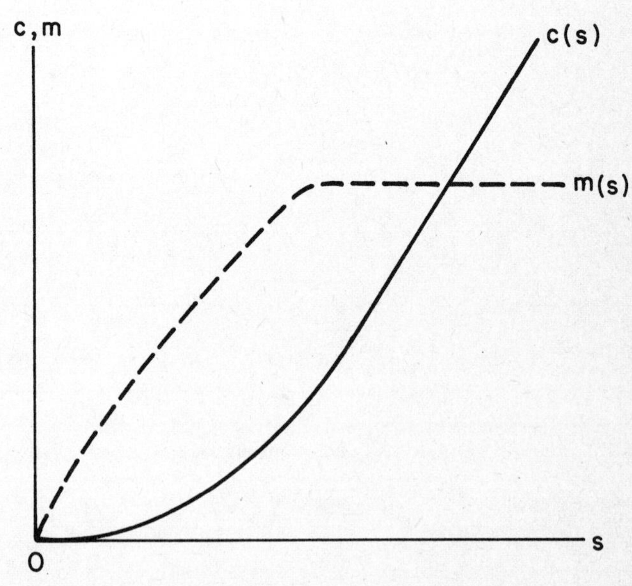

We turn now to a discussion of the properties of the restricted cost function c assuming that it is differentiable with respect to its arguments. The following property is a fundamental one.

The Derivative Property of the Cost Function (Hicks [1946;331], Samuelson [1947;68], Shephard [1953;11]: Let T be given and define c(p,s,k) by (1). Suppose that c is once differentiable with respect to its N price arguments at the point $p^* \gg 0_N$, $s^* \geq 0_I$, $k^* \geq 0_J$. Finally, suppose that x^* solves the cost problem

$$(12) \qquad \min_x \{p^* \cdot x : (x,s^*,k^*) \varepsilon T\} \equiv c(p^*,s^*,k^*).$$

Then x^* is the unique solution to (12) and it is equal to the vector of first order partial derivatives of $c(p^*,s^*,k^*)$ with respect to the components of the price vector; i.e.,

$$(13) \qquad x^* = \nabla_p c(p^*,s^*,k^*).$$

The proof of this property is analogous to the proof of the derivative property of the restricted profit function: the function $g(p) \equiv c(p,s^*,k^*) - p \cdot x$ turns out to be globally maximized at $p = p^*$ and the rest of the proof can readily be adapted.

Thus, if $c(p,s,k)$ is differentiable with respect to the components $p_1,\dots,p_N$ of the price vector p for variable inputs, the government's variable cost minimizing nth input demand function, $x_n(p,s,k)$, can be obtained by partially differentiating $c(p,s,k)$ with respect to p; i.e., we have

$$(14) \qquad x_n(p,s,k) = \partial c(p,s,k)/\partial p_n, \qquad n = 1,2,\dots,N.$$

Property (14) is sometimes called Shephard's Lemma. However, in order to justify (14), we do require that c satisfy Properties 1 and 2 listed above.

Property 1 for c, the linear homogeneity in prices property, Shephard's Lemma (14), and Euler's Theorem on homogeneous functions together imply the following identity:

$$(15) \qquad c(p,s,k) = \Sigma_{n=1}^{N} p_n x_n(p,s,k).$$

The derivation of (15) is analogous to the derivation of (25) in Appendix 1.

Equation (15) also has an important econometric implication: the restricted cost function $c(p,s,k)$ does not contain any additional information that is not already contained in the input demand functions $x_n(p,s,k)$. If the system of N input demand functions (14) were econometrically estimated with error e_n^t in equation n in period t, then the period t error in the cost equation must be equal to $\Sigma_{n=1}^{N} p_n^t e_n^t$, and hence the cost equation would contain no new statistical information. Put in another way, the errors in the system (14) plus (15) would be linearly dependent for each time period t.

If $c(p,s,k)$ is twice continuously differentiable with respect to the components of p, then we may utilize (14) and Properties 1 and 2 for c to derive some additional interesting results. Form the N by N matrix of derivatives of the government variable input demand functions $x_n(p,s,k)$ defined by (14):

$$(16)\qquad \nabla_p x(p,s,k) \equiv \begin{bmatrix} \partial x_1(p,s,k)/\partial p_1, \ldots, \partial x_1(p,s,k)/\partial p_N \\ \vdots \qquad\qquad \vdots \\ \partial x_N(p,s,k)/\partial p_1, \ldots, \partial x_N(p,s,k)/\partial p_N \end{bmatrix}$$

$$= \begin{bmatrix} \partial^2 c(p,s,k)/\partial p_1 \partial p_1, \ldots, \partial^2 c(p,s,k)/\partial p_1 \partial p_N \\ \vdots \qquad\qquad \vdots \\ \partial^2 c(p,s,k)/\partial p_N \partial p_1, \ldots, \partial^2 c(p,s,k)/\partial p_N \partial p_N \end{bmatrix}$$

$$\equiv \nabla^2_{pp} c(p,s,k).$$

We may derive the following restrictions on the matrix of demand derivatives defined by (16):

$$(17)\qquad [\nabla_p x(p,s,k)]^T = [\nabla_p x(p,s,k)],$$

$$(18)\qquad [\nabla_p x(p,s,k)]p = 0_N, \text{ and}$$

$$(19)\qquad \nabla_p x(p,s,k) = \nabla^2_{pp} c(p,s,k) \text{ is a negative semidefinite matrix.}$$

(17) follows from Young's Theorem in the calculus, (18) follows from Property 1 on c and Euler's Theorem on homogeneous functions, and (19) follows from Property 2 on c, the concavity in prices property. (17), (18) and (19) are counterparts to (27), (28) and (29) in Appendix 1. For additional

implications of (17) - (19) above, the reader should refer back to Appendix 1 and modify the more lengthy discussion there to suit the present circumstances.

We now turn to the differentiability properties of $c(p,s,k)$ with respect to the components of the vector of government output variables s. From the definition of a derivative, the partial derivative of $c(p,s,k)$ with respect to s_i is the rate of increase in variable costs with respect to the ith output, holding constant the other outputs and the fixed capital stocks. In economics terminology, $\partial c(p,s,k)/\partial s_i \equiv m_i(p,s,k)$ is the marginal change in cost due to the production of a marginal unit of output i, i.e., $m_i(p,s,k)$ is the government's ith <u>marginal cost function</u>. We may form a vector of these marginal cost functions by partially differentiating $c(p,s,k)$ with respect to the components of s:

$$(20) \qquad m(p,s,k) \equiv \begin{bmatrix} m_1(p,s,k) \\ \vdots \\ m_I(p,s,k) \end{bmatrix} \equiv \begin{bmatrix} \partial c(p,s,k)/\partial s_1 \\ \vdots \\ \partial c(p,s,k)/\partial s_I \end{bmatrix} \equiv \nabla_s c(p,s,k).$$

If the government's production possibilities set T satisfies the free disposal property (5), then the marginal cost functions are nonnegative; i.e., $m(p,s,k) \geq 0_I$.

If $c(p,s,k)$ is twice continuously differentiable with respect to the components of s, then we may differentiate the marginal cost functions defined by (20) with respect to the components of s and we obtain the following symmetry restrictions on this I by I matrix of derivatives:

(21) $$\nabla_s m(p,s,k) = \nabla^2_{ss} c(p,s,k) = [\nabla_s m(p,s,k)]^T$$

The symmetry restrictions (21) are a counterpart to the symmetry restrictions (33) in Appendix 1.

If the government technology set T is convex, then by Proposition 3 above c(p,s,k) is a convex function in the components of s. If c(p,s,k) is also twice continuously differentiable with respect to the components of s, then the matrix of marginal cost derivatives with respect to the components of s will satisfy the following restriction in addition to (21):

(22) $$\nabla_s m(p,s,k) = \nabla^2_{ss} c(p,s,k) \text{ is a positive semidefinite matrix.}$$

Recall that a matrix A is positive semidefinite if and only if $y^T A y \geq 0$ for all $y \neq 0_I$. Thus (22) implies the following I restrictions:

(23) $$\partial m_i(p,s,k)/\partial s_i \geq 0 \qquad \text{for } i = 1,2,\ldots,I.$$

The inequalities (23) tell us that the ith marginal cost function, regarded as a function of the ith output s_i, is upward sloping (or at least it is not downward sloping) and this is true for all i, provided that the government technology set T is convex.

If c(p,s,k) is twice continuously differentiable with respect to both its p and s arguments, then in view of (16) and (20), we obtain the following Samuelson [1953-4] type reciprocity relations:

$$(24)\qquad \nabla_s x(p,s,k) = [\nabla_p m(p,s,k)]^T = \nabla^2_{ps} c(p,s,k).$$

The derivative restrictions (24) are counterparts to the derivative restrictions (36) in Appendix 1. Using the linear homogeneity of $c(p,s,k)$ in p, we may also derive the following counterpart to (41) in Appendix 1:

$$(25)\qquad [\nabla^2_{sp} c(p,s,k)]p = [\nabla_p m(p,s,k)]p = \nabla_s c(p,s,k) = m(p,s,k).$$

We conclude this Appendix by deriving another implication which follows if the government's technology set T is a convex set. Given positive prices $w \equiv (w_1,\ldots,w_I)$ for the I outputs that the government produces, positive input prices $p \equiv (p_1,\ldots,p_N)$ for the N variable inputs and a nonnegative vector $k \equiv (k_1,\ldots,k_J)$ of fixed capital stocks, government production managers may try to choose the vector of outputs s and the vector of variable inputs x which solves the following profit maximization problem:

$$\begin{aligned} &\max_{x,s} \{w\cdot s - p\cdot x : (x,s,k)\varepsilon T\} \\ (26)\qquad &= \max_s \{w\cdot s - c(p,s,k) : s \geq 0_I\} \end{aligned}$$

where the equality (26) follows using the definition (1) of the restricted cost function c.

<u>Proposition 5</u>: Suppose that the government's technology set T is a convex set and satisfies the free disposal property (5). Suppose in addition that the government's restricted cost function c defined by (1) is differentiable with respect to the components of s at (p^*,s^*,k^*). Define the vector of

derivatives of the cost function with respect to the components of the output vector s^* evaluated at (p^*,s^*,k^*) by

$$(27) \qquad w^* \equiv \nabla_s c(p^*,s^*,k^*) \geq 0_I$$

where the inequality in (27) follows from Proposition 2 above. Then s^* is a solution to the following government profit maximization problem:

$$(28) \qquad \max_{x,s} \{w^*\cdot s-p^*\cdot x : (x,s,k^*)\varepsilon T\}$$
$$= \max_s \{w^*\cdot s-c(p^*,s,k^*) : s \geq 0_I\}$$

<u>Proof</u>: Define the function $f(s) \equiv w^*\cdot s-c(p^*,s,k^*)$ for $s \geq 0_I$. Since T is a convex set, by Proposition 3 above, $c(p^*,s,k^*)$ is a convex function of s. Hence $-c(p^*,s,k^*)$ is a concave function as is the linear function of s, $w^*\cdot s$. Since a sum of two concave functions is concave, f(s) is a concave function of s. Since f is concave and differentiable at s^*, the first order Taylor series approximation of f around the point s^* cannot lie below the graph of the function (e.g., see Mangasarian [1969;84] or Varian [1978;253] for a proof of this property), we have

$$f(s) \leq f(s^*) + \nabla f(s^*)\cdot(s-s^*) \quad \text{for all } s \geq 0_I \text{ or}$$

$$(29) \qquad w^*\cdot s-c(p^*,s,k^*) \leq w^*\cdot s^*-c(p^*,s^*,k^*) + \left(w^*-\nabla_s c(p^*,s^*,k^*)\right)\cdot(s-s^*)$$
$$= w^*\cdot s^*-c(p^*,s^*,k^*)$$

where the last equality follows using (27). The inequality (29) shows that the function $w^*\cdot s-c(p^*,s,k^*)$ attains a global max at $s = s^*$. Hence s^* solves (28). Q. E. D.

Proposition 5 shows that the marginal cost equals price system of equations, $\nabla_s c(p,s,k) \equiv m(p,s,k) = w$, can be inverted to give profit maximizing supplies s as functions of (p,w,k). Thus under the hypotheses of Proposition 5, the system of I equations

$$(30) \qquad w = m(p,s,k) \equiv \nabla_s c(p,s,k)$$

may be regarded as a system of inverse supply functions.

<u>Notes</u>

The properties of restricted cost functions were first derived in some detail by McFadden [1966][1978]. A nice exposition of the properties of restricted cost functions may be found in Varian [1978;ch.1]. See also Shephard [1970].

The special case where I=1 so that there is only one output, and J=0, so that all inputs are variable, has a much longer history in economics; see Hicks [1946;331], Samuelson [1947;68] and Shephard [1953].

Complete duality theorems between production possibilities sets T and cost function c have been obtained by a number of authors, including Shephard [1953][1970], McFadden [1966][1978] and Diewert [1971][1982].

Appendix 3. Properties of Restricted Expenditure Functions

We assume that a consumer has preferences defined over combinations of N market goods $x \equiv (x_1,\ldots,x_N)$ which may be bought or sold at positive prices $p \equiv (p_1,\ldots,p_N)$ and combinations of I nonnegative infrastructure services S ≡

$(S_1,\ldots,S_I) \geq 0$ for which there may or may not be user fees. We assume that labour supplies are indexed negatively in the x vector, e.g., if $x_1 < 0$, then the consumer is supplying $-x_1 > 0$ units of that type of labour service. We assume that the consumer's preferences over x, S combinations can be represented by means of a utility function U(x,S). The consumer's <u>restricted</u> or <u>conditional expenditure function</u> e is defined for $p \gg 0_N$ by minimizing the cost of achieving a given utility level u, given that the consumer has available the vector S of infrastructure services, i.e.,

$$(1) \qquad e(u,p,S) \equiv \min_x \{p \cdot x : U(x,S) \geq u\}.$$

We assume that U is sufficiently well behaved so that e is well defined as a minimum.

It is straightforward to show that e(u,p,S) must be a (positively) linearly homogeneous and concave function in the components of p for each fixed u, S (the proof is the same as the proof of Proposition 1 in Appendix 2). Furthermore, if the utility level u increases, then the feasible set of x's for the minimization problem (1) will shrink and so the minimum cannot decrease; i.e., we have $e(u',p,S) \leq e(u'',p,s)$ if $u' < u''$.

If e(u,p,S) is differentiable with respect to the components of p, then the solution to the cost minimization problem (1) is unique and is equal to the vector of first order partial derivatives of e with respect to the components of p; i.e., we have the following analogue to the derivative property of the cost function, (13) in Appendix 2.

$$(2) \qquad x(u,p,S) = \nabla_p e(u,p,S).$$

Let us assume that the utility function U satisfies the following free disposal property with respect to the components of S for every x in the domain of definition of U:

(3) $S'' \geq S' \geq 0_I$ implies $U(x,S'') \geq U(x,S')$ for every x.

Assumption (3) simply tells us that if the consumer gets more infrastructure services, then he or she won't be made worse off. Property (3) on U translates into the following property (4) on the restricted expenditure function e:

(4) $S'' \geq S' \geq 0_I$ implies $e(u,p,S'') \leq e(u,p,S')$;

<u>Proposition 1</u>: Condition (3) on U implies Condition (4) on e.

<u>Proof</u>: Let $S'' \geq S' \geq 0_I$, $p \gg 0_N$ and let u be given with

(5) $$e(u,p,S') \equiv \min_x \{p \cdot x : U(x,S') \geq u\}$$
$$= p \cdot x' \quad \text{with} \quad U(x',S') \geq u.$$

Then using (3), we also have $U(x',S'') \geq u$ and so x' is feasible for the following expenditure minimization problem:

$$e(u,p,S'') \equiv \min_x \{p \cdot x : U(x,S'') \geq u\}$$

$\leq p \cdot x'$ since x' is feasible

$= e(u,p,S')$ using (5). Q. E. D.

We now ask how much a consumer should be willing to pay for an extra unit of the ith type of infrastructure service? If the consumer's initial utility level is u, initial infrastructure services consumption is S and initial net expenditure on market goods is $e(u,p,S)$, then an extra unit of the ith good would enable the consumer to reduce his or her expenditure on market goods to $e(u,p,S_1,S_2,\ldots,S_{i-1},S_i+1,S_{i+1},\ldots,S_I)$. This net reduction in expenditure can be approximated by the following partial derivative in the differentiable case:

(6) $$-\partial e(u,p,S)/\partial S_i \equiv W_i(u,p,S) \geq 0$$

where the inequality in (6) follows if we assume (3) so that e satisfies (4) and so $\partial e(u,p,S)/\partial S_i \leq 0$.

The functions $W_i(u,p,S)$ defined by (6) for $i = 1,\ldots,I$ define the consumer's system of <u>willingness to pay</u> functions which are the consumer analogues to the producer willingness to pay functions defined in Appendix 1.

We shall find it convenient at times to impose the following restrictions on the utility function U:

(7) $$\{(x,S) : U(x,S) \geq u\} \text{ is a closed convex set.}$$

The function U is <u>quasiconcave</u> if (7) is true for all possible utility levels u.

Proposition 2: If U satisfies (7), then e(u,p,S) defined by (1) is a convex function of S.

Proof: Let u be given and suppose U satisfies (7). Let $p \gg 0_N$, $0 \leq \lambda \leq 1$ and let S^1 and S^2 be such that

$$e(u,p,S^i) \equiv \min_x \{p \cdot x : U(x,S^i) \geq u\} = p \cdot x^i \quad \text{for } i = 1,2. \tag{8}$$

Then since (x^1,S^1) and (x^2,S^2) belong to the set defined by (7), so does any convex combination of these points. Thus

$$e(u,p,\lambda S^1 + (1-\lambda)S^2) \equiv \min_x \{p \cdot x : U(x,\lambda S^1 + (1-\lambda)S^2) \geq u\}$$

$$\leq p \cdot (\lambda x^1 + (1-\lambda)x^2)$$

since $\lambda x^1 + (1-\lambda)x^2$ is feasible

$$= \lambda p \cdot x^1 + (1-\lambda)p \cdot x^2$$

$$= \lambda e(u,p,S^1) + (1-\lambda)e(u,p,S^2) \tag{9}$$

using (8).

The inequality (9) establishes the convexity property for e. Q. E. D.

We have the following counterpart to Proposition 5 in Appendix 2.:

Proposition 3: Suppose that the consumer's utility function U satisfies the free disposal property (3) and the convexity property (7) for some utility level u*. Let $p^* \gg 0_N$, $S^* \geq 0_I$ and suppose that the consumer's restricted expenditure function e defined by (1) is differentiable with respect to the components of S at (u*,p*,S*). Define the consumer willingness to pay vector W* by

$$W^* \equiv -\nabla_S e(u^*,p^*,S^*) \geq 0_I. \tag{10}$$

Then S* is a solution to the following consumer minimization problem:

$$\min_{x,S} \{p^*\cdot x + W^*\cdot S : U(x,S) \geq u^*\}$$

$$= \min_S \{e(u^*,p^*,S) + W^*\cdot S : S \geq 0_I\}. \tag{11}$$

The proof of this Proposition is a straightforward modification of the proof of Proposition 5 in Appendix 2. Note that the first order necessary conditions for the minimization problem (11) are equivalent to (10).

The point of Proposition 3 is that under its hypotheses, we can invert the system of willingness to pay functions defined by (6), $W^* = -\nabla_S e(u^*,p^*,S^*)$, into the system of Hicksian demand functions for infrastructure services, $S^* = S(u^*,p^*,W^*)$, which solves (11). Thus under the convexity hypothesis (7) and the free disposal property (3), we may interpret the consumer's system of willingness to pay functions, $W(u,p,S) \equiv -\nabla_S e(u,p,S)$, as a system of inverse Hicksian demand functions for infrastructure services.

Notes

The expenditure function $e(u,p)$ (without the vector of infrastructure services S) and the corresponding system of Hicksian (real income constant) demand functions, $x(u,p) \equiv \nabla_p e(u,p)$, were introduced into the economics literature by Hicks [1946:331]. Restricted cost functions in the production context were studied by McFadden [1978]. Diewert [1978;33] studied the more general function $e(u,p,S)$ defined by (1) and the reader is refered there for a duality theorem and a discussion of some of the finer points about existence and continuity. Diewert [1978] shows that $e(u,p,S)$ is jointly convex in u and S for fixed p if and only if $U(x,S)$ is jointly concave in x and S. Propositions 2 and 3 above appear to be "new" results.

Appendix 4. Proofs of Propositions

Proof of Proposition 1: Since $\pi(p,s)$ defined by (38) is quadratic in s for each fixed p, its second order Taylor series expansion will be exact. Thus we have:

$$\pi(p^0,s^1) - \pi(p^0,s^0) = \nabla_s\pi(p^0,s^0)\cdot(s^1-s^0) + (1/2)(s^1-s^0)\cdot\nabla^2_{ss}\pi(p^0,s^0)(s^1-s^0)$$

(1) $$= w^0\cdot(s^1-s^0) + (b\cdot p^0)(1/2)(s^1-s^0)\cdot A(s^1-s^0) \text{ and}$$

(2) $$\pi(p^1,s^0) - \pi(p^1,s^1) = \nabla_s\pi(p^1,s^1)\cdot(s^0-s^1) + (1/2)(s^0-s^1)\cdot\nabla^2_{ss}\pi(p^1,s^1)(s^0-s^1)$$

$$= w^1\cdot(s^0-s^1) + (b\cdot p^1)(1/2)(s^0-s^1)\cdot A(s^0-s^1).$$

(2) may be rearranged to read as follows:

$$\text{(3)}\qquad \pi(p^1,s^1) - \pi(p^1,s^0)$$
$$= w^1\cdot(s^1-s^0) - (b\cdot p^1)(1/2)(s^1-s^0)\cdot A(s^0-s^1).$$

Divide both sides of (1) through by $b\cdot p^0$ and divide both sides of (3) through by $b\cdot p^1$. Now take an average of the resulting two equations and obtain (39), making use of definitions (40) and the linear homogeneity in prices property of the restricted profit function π defined by (38). Q. E. D.

Proof of Proposition 2: In order to solve the system of equations (41) - (43), we would expect $\pi(p,s)$ to have at least $1 + (N+I) + (N+I)^2$ independent parameters. However, if π and π^* are both twice continuously differentiable at (p^*,s^*), Young's Theorem on the symmetry of second order partial derivatives (see equations (27), (33) and (36) in Appendix 1) reduces the number of independent second order derivatives from $(N+I)^2$ to $N(N+1)/2 + NI + I(I+1)/2$. The linear homogeneity of π and π^* imply the following additional $1+N+I$ restrictions on the derivatives of π and π^* (recall equations (25), (28) and (41) in Appendix 1):

$$\text{(4)}\qquad \pi(p^*,s^*) = p^*\cdot\nabla_p\pi(p^*,s^*),$$

$$\text{(5)}\qquad [\nabla^2_{pp}\pi(p^*,s^*)]p^* = 0_N, \text{ and}$$

$$\text{(6)}\qquad [\nabla^2_{sp}\pi(p^*,s^*)]p^* = \nabla_s\pi(p^*,s^*).$$

In view of all of these restrictions on both π and π^*, we see that π will have to have at least $N(N+1)/2 + NI + I(I+1)/2$ independent parameters.

Let $b \equiv (b_1,\ldots,b_N) > 0_N$ be any given vector which is nonnegative and nonzero, and consider the following special case of (38):

$$(7)\qquad \pi(p,s) \equiv \Sigma_{n=1}^{N} p_n c_n + (1/2)\Sigma_{m=1}^{N-1}\Sigma_{n=1}^{N-1} c_{mn} p_m p_n p_N^{-1} + \Sigma_{n=1}^{N}\Sigma_{i=1}^{I} b_{ni} p_n s_i + (1/2)\Sigma_{n=1}^{N} b_n p_n \Sigma_{i=1}^{I}\Sigma_{j=1}^{I} a_{ij} s_i s_j$$

where $a_{ij} = a_{ji}$ for all i and j and the N-1 by N-1 matrix of the c_{mn} is symmetric and positive semidefinite. Under these restrictions, it can be verified that $\pi(p,s)$ is linearly homogeneous and convex in p. Since the b_n parameters are determined already, $\pi(p,s)$ defined by (7) has N independent c_n parameters, $N(N-1)/2$ independent c_{mn} parameters, NI independent b_{ni} parameters and $I(I+1)/2$ independent a_{ij} parameters. This is the minimal number of parameters required to satisfy equations (41) - (43).

Solve the following system for the a_{ij}, $1 \leq i \leq j \leq I$:

$$(8)\qquad \partial^2\pi(p^*,s^*)/\partial s_i\partial s_j = (\Sigma_{n=1}^{N} b_n p_n^*)a_{ij} = \partial^2\pi^*(p^*,s^*)/\partial s_i\partial s_j.$$

With the a_{ij} determined, solve (9) for the b_{ni}, $n = 1,\ldots,N, i = 1,\ldots,I$:

$$(9)\qquad \partial^2\pi(p^*,s^*)/\partial p_n\partial s_i = b_{ni} + b_n\Sigma_{j=1}^{I} a_{ij}s_j^* = \partial^2\pi^*(p^*,s^*)/\partial p_n\partial s_i.$$

Now solve the following system of equations for the c_{mn} for $1 \leq m < n \leq$ N-1:

(10) $$\partial^2\pi(p^*,s^*)/\partial p_m \partial p_n = c_{mn}p_N^{*-1} = \partial^2\pi^*(p^*,s^*)/\partial p_m \partial p_n.$$

Now solve the N-1 equations (11) for c_{nn}, n = 1,2,...,N-1:

(11) $$\partial^2\pi(p^*,s^*)/\partial p_N \partial p_n = -\Sigma_{m=1}^{N-1} c_{mn}p_m^* p_N^{*-2} = \partial^2\pi^*(p^*,s^*)/\partial p_N \partial p_n.$$

All of the parameters of π defined by (7) have now been determined with the exception of the N c_n's. Use (12) below to solve for c_n for n = 1,2,..., N-1:

(12) $$\partial\pi(p^*,s^*)/\partial p_n = c_n + \Sigma_{m=1}^{N-1} c_{mn}p_m^*(p_N^*)^{-1} + \Sigma_{i=1}^{I} b_{ni}s_i^* + (1/2)b_n\Sigma_{i=1}^{I}\Sigma_{j=1}^{I} a_{ij}s_i^*s_j^* = \partial\pi^*(p^*,s^*)/\partial p_n.$$

Finally, c_N is determined by solving the following equation:

(13) $$\partial\pi(p^*,s^*)/\partial p_N = c_N - (1/2)\Sigma_{m=1}^{N-1}\Sigma_{n=1}^{N-1} c_{mn}p_m^*p_n^*(p_N^*)^{-2} + \Sigma_{i=1}^{I} b_{Ni}s_i^* + (1/2)b_N\Sigma_{i=1}^{I}\Sigma_{j=1}^{I} a_{ij}s_i^*s_j^* = \partial\pi^*(p^*,s^*)/\partial p_N.$$

The remaining equations in the system (41) - (43) turn out to be satisfied, using the symmetry of the second order partial derivatives of π and π^* and using the restrictions (4) - (6) above. Q. E. D.

Proof of Proposition 3: If p_N is fixed, then $\pi(p,s)$ defined by (44) is quadratic in $p_1,p_2,\ldots,p_{N-1}$ and thus its second order Taylor series expansion in p will be exact for each fixed s. Thus we have:

$$\pi(p^1/p_N^1,s^0) = \pi(p^0/p_N^0,s^0) + \nabla_p\pi(p^0/p_N^0,s^0)\cdot[(p^1/p_N^1) - (p^0/p_N^0)]$$

$$+ (1/2)[(p^1/p_N^1) - (p^0/p_N^0)]\cdot\nabla_{pp}^2\pi(p^0/p_N^0,s^0)[(p^1/p_N^1) - (p^0/p_N^0)]$$

$$= (p^0/p_N^0)\cdot x^0 + x^0\cdot[(p^1/p_N^1) - (p^0/p_N^0)]$$

$$+ (1/2)\Sigma_{m=1}^{N-1}\Sigma_{n=1}^{N-1}c_{mn}[(p_m^1/p_N^1) - (p_m^0/p_N^0)][(p_n^1/p_N^1) - (p_n^0/p_N^0)]$$

(14) $$\equiv (p^1/p_N^1)\cdot x^0 + (1/2)\gamma$$

where we have used (26) and (31) and definition (44). Similarly, we have

$$\pi(p^0/p_N^0,s^1) = \pi(p^1/p_N^1,s^1) + \nabla_p\pi(p^1/p_N^1,s^1)\cdot[(p^0/p_N^0) - (p^1/p_N^1)]$$

$$+ (1/2)[(p^0/p_N^0)-(p^1/p_N^1)]\cdot\nabla_{pp}^2\pi(p^1/p_N^1,s^1)[(p^0/p_N^0)-(p^1/p_N^1)]$$

$$= (p^1/p_N^1)\cdot x^1 + x^1\cdot[(p^0/p_N^0) - (p^1/p_N^1)]$$

$$+ (1/2)\Sigma_{m=1}^{N-1}\Sigma_{n=1}^{N-1}c_{mn}[(p_m^1/p_N^1) - (p_m^0/p_N^0)][(p_n^1/p_N^1) - (p_n^0/p_N^0)]$$

(15) $$= (p^0/p_N^0)\cdot x^1 + (1/2)\gamma.$$

Thus

$$\pi(p^0/p_N^0,s^1) - \pi(p^0/p_N^0,s^0)$$

(16) $$= (p^0/p_N^0)\cdot(x^1-x^0) + (1/2)\gamma$$ using (15) and (26);

$$\pi(p^1/p_N^1,s^1) - \pi(p^1/p_N^1,s^0)$$

$$= (p^1/p_N^1)\cdot x^1 - \{(p^1/p_N^1)\cdot x^0 + (1/2)\gamma\}$$ using (26) and (14)

(17) $$= (p^1/p_N^1)\cdot(x^1-x^0) - (1/2)\gamma.$$

Taking an average of (16) and (17) establishes (45). Q. E. D.

Proof of Proposition 4: The functional form for $\pi(p,s)$ defined by (7) above in the proof of Proposition 2 is also a member of the class of functions defined by (44). Hence the proof of Proposition 2 provides a proof of the present Proposition. Q. E. D.

Proof of Proposition 5: Introduce a nonnegative vector $q \geq 0_M$ of Lagrange-Kuhn-Tucker multipliers for the inequality constraints in the constrained maximization problem (55). Let us also assume that a feasible solution for (55) exists which satisfies each inequality constraint with a strict inequality. Then we may apply the Karlin [1959;201]-Uzawa [1958;34] Saddle Point Theorem and rewrite (55) as the following max min problem:

$$B = \max_{x^0, x^1,\ldots,x^F,y^0,y^1,\ldots y^F} \min_{q\geq 0_M} \{p\cdot[\Sigma_{f=1}^F x^f - x^0]$$

$$- p\cdot[\Sigma_{f=1}^F x^{f0} - x^{00}] + q\cdot[\Sigma_{f=1}^F y^f - y^0] - q\cdot[\Sigma_{f=1}^F y^{f0} - y^{00}] :$$

$$(x^0,y^0,s^{11},\ldots,s^{F1},k^0)\varepsilon T^0 \ ; \ (x^f,y^f,s^{f1},k^f)\varepsilon T^f, f = 1,\ldots,F\}$$

$$= \min_{q \geq 0_M} \{\Sigma_{f=1}^F \pi^f(p,q,s^{f1},k^f) - c(p,q,s^{11},\ldots,s^{F1},k^0)$$

$$-p\cdot[\Sigma_{f=1}^F s^{f0} - x^{00}] + q\cdot[\Sigma_{f=1}^F y^{f0} - y^{00}]\}$$

using definitions (51) and (52) in the main text.

The corollaries follow using the Kuhn-Tucker [1951] conditions for the convex programming problem defined by (56) (see Karlin [1959;204] for a convenient exposition of the Kuhn-Tucker conditions.) Q. E. D.

Proof of Proposition 6: Using assumption (53) and definition (51),

$$\pi^f(p,q^1,s^{f0},k^f) \equiv \max_{x,y} \{p\cdot x+q^1\cdot y : (x,y,s^{f0},k^f)\varepsilon T^f\}$$

$$(18) \qquad \geq p\cdot x^{f0} + q^1\cdot y^{f0}, \qquad f = 1,\ldots,F$$

since (x^{f0},y^{f0}) is feasible for the firm f maximization problem. Similarly, using assumption (54) and definition (52),

$$c(p,q^1,s^{10},\ldots,s^{F0},k^0) \equiv \min_{x,y} \{p\cdot x+q^1\cdot y : (x,y,s^{10},\ldots,s^{F0},k^0)\varepsilon T^0\}$$

$$(19) \qquad \leq p\cdot x^{00} + q^1\cdot y^{00}$$

since (x^{00},y^{00}) is feasible for the minimization problem. Using definition (61),

$$B^1 \equiv \Sigma_{f=1}^{F}\{\pi^f(p,q^1,s^{f1},k^f) - \pi^f(p,q^1,s^{f0},k^f)\}$$

$$- \{c(p,q^1,s^{11},\ldots,s^{F1},k^0) - c(p,q^1s^{10},\ldots,s^{F0},k^0)\}$$

$$\leq \Sigma_{f=1}^{F}\{\pi^f(p,q^1,s^{f1},k^f) - [p\cdot x^{f0}+q^1\cdot y^{f0}]\}$$

$$- \{c(p,q^1,s^{11},\ldots,s^{F1},k^0) - [p\cdot x^{00}+q^1\cdot y^{00}]\}$$

using (18) and (19)

$$\equiv B.$$

This establishes one half of (62). The other half may be established as follows:

(20) $$\max_{x^0,x^1,\ldots,x^F,y^0,y^1,\ldots,y^F}\{p\cdot[\Sigma_{f=1}^{F}x^f-x^0] + q^0\cdot[\Sigma_{f=1}^{F}y^f-y^0]$$

$$- p\cdot[\Sigma_{f=1}^{F}x^{f0}-x^{00}] - q^0\cdot[\Sigma_{f=1}^{F}y^{f0}-y^{00}] : (x^0,y^0,s^{11},\ldots,s^{F1},k^0)\varepsilon T^0;$$

$$(x^f,y^f,s^{f1},k^f)\varepsilon T^f \;;\; f = 1,\ldots,F\}$$

$$= \Sigma_{f=1}^{F}\pi^f(p,q^0,s^{f1},k^f) - c(p,q^0,s^{11},\ldots{}^{F1},k^0) - p\cdot[\Sigma_{f=1}^{F}x^{f0}-x^{00}]$$

$$- q^0\cdot[\Sigma_{f=1}^{F}y^{f0}-y^{00}]$$

using definitions (51) and (52)

$$= \Sigma_{f=1}^{F}\{\pi^f(p,q^0,s^{f1},k^f) - \pi^f(p,q^0,s^{f0},k^f)\}$$

$$- \{c(p,q^0,s^{11},\ldots,s^{F1},k^0) - c(p,q^0,\ldots,s^{F0},k^0)\}$$

using assumptions (53) and (54)

$$\equiv B^0 \qquad \text{using definition (60)}$$

(21) $$\geq \max_{x^0,x^1,\ldots,x^F,y^0,y^1,\ldots,y^F} \{p\cdot[\Sigma_{f=1}^F x^f - x^0] + q^0\cdot[\Sigma_{f=1}^F y^f - y^0]$$

$$- p\cdot[\Sigma_{f=1}^F x^{f0} - x^{00}] - q^0\cdot[\Sigma_{f=1}^F y^{f0} - y^{00}] : \Sigma_{f=1}^F y^f - y^0 \geq \Sigma_{f=1}^F y^{f0} - y^{00};$$

$$(x^0,y^0,s^{11},\ldots,s^{F1},k^0)\varepsilon T^0 \;;\; (x^f,y^f,s^{f1},k^f)\varepsilon T^f \;;\; f = 1,\ldots,F\}$$

since we have added the constraints $\Sigma_{f=1}^F y^f - y^0 \geq \Sigma_{f=1}^F y^{f0} - y^{00}$ to the constrained maximization problem (20) and thus the maximum for the more constrained problem (21) cannot increase

$$\geq p\cdot[\Sigma_{f=1}^F x^{f1} - x^{01}] + q^0\cdot[\Sigma_{f=1}^F y^{f1} - y^{01}] - p\cdot[\Sigma_{f=1}^F x^{f0} - x^{00}] - q^0\cdot[\Sigma_{f=1}^F y^{f0} - y^{00}]$$

where $x^{01},x^{11},\ldots,x^{F1},y^{01},y^{11},\ldots,y^{F1}$ is a solution to (55) and hence is feasible for the constrained maximization problem (21)

$$= B + q^0\cdot[\Sigma_{f-1}^F y^{f1} - y^{01}] - q^0\cdot[\Sigma_{f=1}^F y^{f0} - y^{00}]$$

since B defined by (59) is equal to the optimized objective for (55), $p\cdot[\Sigma_{f=1}^{F}x^{f1}-x^{01}] - p\cdot[\Sigma_{f=1}^{F}x^{f0}-x^{00}]$

$= B$ since $q^1 \gg 0_N$ implies $\Sigma_{f=1}^{F}y^{f1}-y^{01} = \Sigma_{f=1}^{F}y^{f0}-y^{00}$. Q. E. D.

Proof of Proposition 7: Doing a first order approximation for B^0 around the s^{f0} allocation means that we treat the s^{f1} as variables, differentiate B^0 defined by (60) with respect to the components of the vector s^{f1}, evaluate the resulting vector of derivatives at $s^{f1} = s^{f0}$ and take the inner product of the vector of derivatives with $(s^{f1} - s^{f0})$. Finally, sum these inner products over f and establish that B^0 is approximated to the first order by expression (62).

Establishing that B* is approximated by (62) is more complicated. When we differentiate B* defined by (59), it is necessary to remember that the price vector q^1 is also a function of $s^{11},\ldots,s^{F1}$. Assuming that $q^1 \gg 0_M$, q^1 is the solution to (57) where the inequalities there are replaced by equalities. Totally differentiating these equations at the initial equilibrium where $q^1 = q^0$ yields the following expression for the derivative matrices of q with respect to the elements of s^f, $\nabla_{s^f}q(s^1,\ldots,s^F)$:

$$[\Sigma_{f=1}^{F}\nabla^2_{qq}\pi^f(p,q^0,s^{f0},k^f) - \nabla^2_{qq}c(p,q^0s^{10},\ldots,s^{F0},k^0)][\nabla_{s^1}q,\ldots,\nabla_{s^F}q]$$

(22) $$= - [\nabla^2_{qs^1}\pi^1(p,q^0,s^{10},k^1) - \nabla^2_{qs^1}c(p,q^0,s^{10},\ldots,s^{F0},k^0),\ldots,$$

$$\nabla^2_{qs^F}\pi^F(p,q^0,s^{F0},k^F) - \nabla^2_{qs^F}c(p,q^0,s^{10},\ldots,s^{F0},k^0)].$$

We assume that the M by M matrix on the left hand side of (22) is positive definite (it must be positive semidefinite by the properties of restricted profit and cost functions) and hence, by the Implicit Function Theorem, $q(s^{11},\ldots,s^{F1})$ exists, at least for s^{1f} close to s^{f0}. Now differentiate B* defined by (59) with respect to s^{f1} and evaluate the resulting derivatives at $s^{f0} = s^{f1}$. Under these conditions, we have $q^1 = q^0$ and we obtain the following derivatives for f = 1,2,...,F:

$$\nabla_{s^{f1}}B^* = \nabla_{s^f}\pi^f(p,q^0,s^{f0},k^f) - \nabla_{s^f}c(p,q^0,s^{10},\ldots,s^{F0},k^0)$$

$$+ \{\Sigma_{f=1}^F\nabla_q\pi^f(p,q^0,s^{f0},k^f) - \nabla_q c(p,q^0,s^{10},\ldots,s^{F0},k^0)$$

$$- \Sigma_{f=1}^F y^{f0}+y^{00}\}\cdot\nabla_{s^f}q(s^{10},\ldots,s^{F0})$$

(23) $$= \nabla_{s^f}\pi^f(p,q^0,s^{f0},k^f) - \nabla_{s^f}c(p,q^0,s^{10},\ldots,s^{F0},k^0)$$

since the term in brackets is 0_M using the equality version of (57)

$$\equiv w^{f0} - m^{f0}.$$

Note that when $s^{f1} = s^{f0}$ and $q^1 = q^0$, we have B* = 0. Thus, a first order approximation to B* around the s^{f0} allocation using (23) is

$$B^* \simeq \Sigma_{f=1}^{F}\{w^{f0} - m^{f0}\}\cdot\{s^{f1} - s^{f0}\} \qquad \text{which is (62)} \qquad \text{Q. E. D.}$$

Proof of Proposition 8: Using the same notation as in the proof of the previous proposition, it is straightforward to show that the second order approximation to B^0 around the point $s^{10},s^{20},\ldots s^{F0}$ is the right hand side of (24) below:

$$(24) \qquad B^0 \simeq \Sigma_{f=1}^{F}[w^{f0}-m^{f0}]\cdot[s^{f1}-s^{f0}] + (1/2)\Sigma_{f=1}^{F}\Sigma_{g=1}^{F}[s^{f1}-s^{f0}]\cdot\{\nabla^2_{s^f s^g}\pi^f(p,q^0,s^{f0},k^f) - \nabla^2_{s^f s^g}c(p,q,{}^0,s^{10},\ldots,s^{F0},k^0)\}[s^{g1}-s^{g0}].$$

$$(25) \qquad \equiv \Sigma_{f=1}^{F}[w^{f0}-m^{f0}]\cdot[s^{f1}-s^{f0}] + \beta.$$

Note that if the private and public production possibilities sets T^f and T^0 are convex, then by Propostion 3 in Appendices 1 and 2 above, we can deduce that β, the second set of terms on the right hand side of (24) will always be negative or zero. Hence, under the convexity hypothesis, the second order approximation to B^0 will generally give a smaller measure of benefits than the corresponding first order approximation.

To form the second order approximation to B*, we need only to differentiate the terms defined by (23) above, recognizing that q is a function of $s^1,\ldots,s^F$. We find that the second order approximation to B* around the initial infrastructure services allocation is the right hand side of (26) below:

(26) $$B^* \simeq \Sigma_{f=1}^{F}[w^{f0}-m^{f0}]\cdot[s^{f1}-s^{f0}] + \beta$$

$$+ (1/2)\Sigma_{f=1}^{F}\Sigma_{g=1}^{F}[s^{f1}-s^{f0}]\cdot[\nabla^2_{s^fq}\pi^f(p,q^0,s^{f0},k^f)[s^{g1}-s^{g0}]$$

$$- \nabla^2_{s^fq}c(p,q^0,s^{10},\ldots,s^{F0},k^0)]\nabla_{s^g}q(s^{10},\ldots,s^{F0})$$

where β is defined by (25) and $\nabla_{s^g}q$ is defined by (22)

$$= \Sigma_{f=1}^{F}[w^{f0}-m^{f0}]\cdot[s^{f1}-s^{f0}] + \beta$$

$$- (1/2)\Sigma_{f=1}^{F}\Sigma_{g=1}^{F}[s^{f1}-s^{f0}]\cdot[\nabla^2_{s^fq}\pi^f-\nabla^2_{s^fq}c][\Sigma_{f=1}^{F}\nabla^2_{qq}\pi^f-\nabla^2_{qq}c]^{-1}\cdot$$

$$[\nabla^2_{qs^g}\pi^g(p,q^0,s^{g0},k) - \nabla^2_{qs^g}c(p,q^0s^{10},\ldots,s^{F0},k^0)][s^{g1}-s^{g0}]$$

using (22)

(27) $$\leq \Sigma_{f=1}^{F}[w^{f0}-m^{f0}]\cdot[s^{f1}-s^{f0}] + \beta$$

where the inequality follows using the positive definiteness of the matrix $[\Sigma_{f=1}^{F}\nabla^2_{qq}\pi^f(p,q^0,s^{f0},k^f) - \nabla^2_{qq}c(p,q^0,s^{10},\ldots,s^{F0},k^0]$. The inequality (27) is actually a consequence of Samuelson's [1947;36-39] Le Chatelier Principle.

Q. E. D.

<u>Proof of Proposition 9</u>: The proof is analogous to the proof of Proposition 5. Q. E. D.

<u>Proof of Proposition 10</u>: The proof is analogous to the proof of Proposition 6. Q. E. D.

<u>Proof of Proposition 11</u>: The proof is analogous to the proof of Proposition 7 except that our old assumption that the M by M matrix on the left hand side of (22) was positive definite is now replaced by the following assumption:

$$(28)\qquad \Big[\Sigma_{f=1}^{F}\nabla_{qq}^{2}\pi^{f}(p,q^{0},s^{f0},k^{f}) - \nabla_{qq}^{2}c(p,q^{0},s^{10},\ldots,s^{F0},S^{10},\ldots,S^{H0},k^{0}) - \Sigma_{h=1}^{H}\nabla_{qq}^{2}m^{h}(u_{0}^{h},p,q^{0},S^{h0})\Big] \text{ is a positive definite matrix.}$$

We also require the hypotheses listed in Proposition (9) and the existence of the various derivatives of π^{f}, c and the m^{h}. Q. E. D.

<u>Proof of Proposition 12</u>: The proof follows in the same manner as the proof of Proposition 8. To find the second order approximation to B^{0}, <u>add</u> the following terms to the right hand side of (24):

$$(29)\qquad \Sigma_{h=1}^{H}(W^{h0}-M^{h0})\cdot(S^{h1}-S^{h0}) + (1/2)\Sigma_{h=1}^{H}\Sigma_{k=1}^{H}(S^{h1}-S^{h0})\cdot\{-\nabla_{S^{h}S^{k}}^{2}m^{h}(u_{h}^{0},p,q^{0},S^{h0}) - \nabla_{S^{h}S^{k}}^{2}c(p,q^{0},s^{10},\ldots,s^{F0},S^{10},\ldots,S^{H0},k^{0})\}\{S^{k1}-S^{k0}\} + \Sigma_{f=1}^{F}\Sigma_{h=1}^{H}(s^{f1}-s^{f0})\cdot\{-\nabla_{s^{f}S^{h}}^{2}c(p,q^{0},s^{10},\ldots,s^{F0},S^{10},\ldots,S^{H0},k^{0})\}\{S^{h1}-S^{h0}\}.$$

To find the second order approximation to B*, add to the right hand side of (26) the terms defined by (29) above and the additional terms, where all of the matrices of derivatives are evaluated at the data for the initial 0 equilibrium:

$$(30) \quad -(1/2)\Sigma_{f=1}^{F}\Sigma_{i=1}^{F}(s^{f1}-s^{f0})\cdot(\nabla^2_{s^f q}\pi^f-\nabla^2_{s^f q}c)A^{-1}(\nabla^2_{qs^i}\pi^i-\nabla^2_{qs^i}c)(s^{i1}-s^{i0})$$

$$-(1/2)\Sigma_{h=1}^{H}\Sigma_{k=1}^{H}(s^{h1}-s^{h0})\cdot(-\nabla^2_{s^h q}m^h-\nabla^2_{s^h q}c)A^{-1}(-\nabla^2_{qs^k}m^k-\nabla^2_{qs^k}c)(s^{k1}-s^{k0})$$

$$-\Sigma_{f=1}^{F}\Sigma_{h=1}^{H}(s^{f1}-s^{f0})\cdot(\nabla^2_{s^f q}\pi^f-\nabla^2_{s^f q}c)A^{-1}(-\nabla^2_{qs^h}m^h-\nabla^2_{qs^h}c)(s^{h1}-s^{h0}) \le 0$$

$$\le 0$$

where A is the matrix defined by (28) and the inequality in (30) follows from the positive definiteness of A. Q. E. D.

REFERENCES

Allais, M. (1977), "Theories of General Economic Equilibrium and Maximum Efficiency," pp.129-201 in Equilibrium and Disequilibrium in Economic Theory, E. Schwoediauer (ed.), Dordrecht: D. Reidel.

Allais, M. (1943), A la recherche d'une discipline économique, Tome I, Paris: Imprimerie Nationale.

Appelbaum, E. (1979), "Testing Price Taking Behaviour," Journal of Econometrics 9, pp.283-294.

Appelbaum, E., and U. R. Kohli (1979), "Canada-United States Trade: Tests for the Small-Open-Economy Hypotheses," Canadian Journal of Economics 12, pp.1-14.

Auerbach, A. J. (1982), "The Theory of Excess Burden and Optimal Taxation," Working Paper #1025, National Bureau of Economic Research, Cambridge, Massachusetts, November.

Arrow, K. J. (1964), "Control in Large Organizations," Management Science 10, pp.397-408.

Barnett, W. A. (1983), "New Indices of Money Supply and the Flexible Laurent Demand System," Journal of Business and Economic Statistics 1, pp.7-23.

Berndt and Wood (1979), "Engineering and Econometric Interpretations of Energy-Capital Complementarity," The American Economic Review 69, pp.342-354.

Blackorby, C., D. Primont, and R. R. Russell (1978), Duality, Separability, and Functional Structure: Theory and Economic Applications, New York: Elsevier North-Holland.

Blackorby, C., and W. Schworm (1982), "Aggregate Investment and Consistent Intertemporal Technologies," Review of Economic Studies 49, pp.595-614.

Blackorby, C., and W. Schworm (1983a), "Aggregating Heterogeneous Capital Goods in Adjustment-Cost Technologies," Scandinavian Journal of Economics 85, pp.207-222.

Blackorby, C., and W. Schworm (1983b), "The Existence of Labour Aggregates in a Competitive Economy," Discussion Paper 83-34, Department of Economics, The University of British Columbia, Vancouver, Canada.

Blackorby, C., and W. Schworm (1984), "The Structure of Economies with Aggregate Measures of Capital: A Complete Characterization," Discussion Paper 84-03, Department of Economics, The University of British Columbia, Vancouver, Canada.

Bowley, A. L. (1928), "Notes on Index Numbers," Economic Journal 38, pp.216-237.

Binswanger, H. P. (1974), "The Measurement of Technical Change Biases with Many Factors of Production," American Economic Review 64, pp.964-976.

Binswanger, H. P., and V. L. Ruttan (eds.) (1978), Induced Innovation: Technology, Institutions and Development, Baltimore: Johns Hopkins University Press.

Bliss, C. J. (1975), Capital Theory and the Distribution of Income, Amsterdam: North-Holland.

Christensen, L. R., D Cummings, and P. E. Schoech (1983), "Econometric Estimation of Scale Economies in Telecommunications," pp.27-53 in Economic Analysis of Telecommunications, L. Courville, A. DeFontenay and R. Dobell (eds.), Amsterdam: North-Holland.

Christensen, L. R., and D. W. Jorgenson (1973), "Measuring the Performance of the Private Sector of the U. S. Economy, 1929-1969," pp.233-351 in M. Moss (ed.), Measuring Economic and Social Performance, New York: University Press.

Christensen, L. R., D. W. Jorgenson, and L. J. Lau (1971), "Conjugate Duality and the Transcendental Logarithmic Production Function," Econometrica 39, pp.255-256.

Copithorne, L. W. (1976), "La théorie des prix de transfert internes des grandes societiétés," L'actualité économique 52, pp.324-352.

Caves, D. W., L. R. Christensen, and W. E. Diewert (1982), "The Economic Theory of Index Numbers and the Measurement of Input, Output and Productivity," Econometrica 50, pp.1393-1414.

Dantzig, G. B. (1963), Linear Programming and Extensions, Princeton, N.J.: Princeton University Press.

Debreu, G. (1951), "The Coefficient of Resource Utilization," Econometrica 19, pp.273-292.

Debreu, G. (1954), "A Classical Tax-Subsidy Problem," Econometrica 22, 14-22.

Denny, M., C. Everson, M. Fuss, and L. Waverman (1981), "Estimating the Effects of Diffusion of Techological Innovations in Telecommunications: The Production Structure of Bell Canada," Canadian Journal of Economics 14, pp.24-43.

Diewert, W. E. (1969), "Functional Form in the Theory of Production and Consumer Demand," Ph.D. dissertation, University of California, Berkeley, California.

Diewert, W. E. (1971), "An Application of the Shephard Duality Theorem: A Generalized Leontief Production Function," Journal of Political Economy 79, pp.481-507.

Diewert, W. E. (1973), "Functional Forms for Profit and Transformation Functions," Journal of Economic Theory 6, pp.284-316.

Diewert, W. E. (1974), "Applications of Duality Theory," pp.106-171 in Frontiers of Quantitative Economics, Vol. II, M. D. Intriligator and D. A. Kenrick (eds.), Amsterdam: North-Holland.

Diewert, W. E. (1976), "Exact and Superlative Index Numbers," Journal of Econometrics 4, pp.115-145.

Diewert, W. E. (1978), "Hicks Aggregation Theorem and the Existence of a Real Value Added Function," pp.17-51 in Production Economics: A Dual Approach to Theory and Applications, M. Fuss and D. McFadden (eds.), Amsterdam: North-Holland.

Diewert, W. E. (1980), "Aggregation Problems in the Measurement of Capital," pp.433-528 in The Measurement of Capital, Dan Usher (ed.), Chicago: The University of Chicago Press.

Diewert, W. E. (1981a), "The Measurement of Deadweight Loss Revisited," Econometrica 49, pp.1225-1244.

Diewert, W. E. (1981b), "The Economic Theory of Index Numbers: A Survey," pp.163-208 in Essays in the Theory and Measurement of Consumer Behaviour in Honour of Sir Richard Stone, A. Deaton (ed.) London: Cambridge University Press.

Diewert, W. E. (1982), "Duality Approaches to Microeconomic Theory," pp.535-599 in K. J. Arrow and M. D. Intriligator (eds.), Handbook of Mathematical Economics, Vol. 2, Amsterdam: North-Holland.

Diewert, W. E. (1983a), "Cost-Benefit Analysis and Project Evaluation: A Comparison of Alternative Approaches," Journal of Public Economics 22, pp.265-302.

Diewert, W. E. (1983b), "The Measurement of Waste within the Production Sector of an Open Economy," Scandinavian Journal of Economics 85, pp.159-179.

Diewert, W. E. (1983c), "The Theory of the Output Price Index and the Measurement of Real Output Change," pp.1049-1113 in Price Level Measurement, W. E. Diewert and C. Montmarquette (eds.) Ottawa: Statistics Canada.

Diewert, W. E. (1984a), "The Measurement of Deadweight Loss in an Open Economy," Economica 51, pp.23-42.

Diewert, W. E. (1984b), "On the Relationship between the Measurement of Deadweight Loss and the Measurement of Project Benefits," Discussion Paper 84-32, Department of Economics, University of British Columbia, Vancouver, Canada.

Diewert, W. E. (1985a), "Transfer Pricing and Economic Efficiency," pp.47-81 in Multinationals and Transfer Pricing, A. M. Rugman and L. Eden (eds.), London: Croom Helm.

Diewert, W. E. (1985b), "A Dynamic Approach to the Measurement of Waste in an Open Economy," Journal of International Economics, forthcoming.

Diewert, W. E. (1985c), "The Measurement of Waste and Welfare in Applied General Equilibrium Models," forthcoming in a volume edited by John Pigott and John Whalley, Cambridge University Press.

Diewert, W. E., and T. R. Lewis (1982), "The Comparative Dynamics of Efficient Programs of Capital Accumulation and Resource Depletion," pp.301-325 in Economic Theory of Natural Resources, W. Eichhorn, R. Henn, K. Neumann and R. W. Shephard, (eds.), Vienna: Physica-Verlag.

Diewert, W. E., A. H. Turunen, and A. D. Woodland (1984), "Productivity and Pareto Improving Changes in Taxes and Tariffs," Discussion Paper 84-06, Department of Economics, University of British Columbia, Vancouver, Canada.

Diewert, W. E., and T. J. Wales (1984), "Flexible Functional Forms and Global Curvature Conditions," Technical Working Paper No. 40, National Bureau of Economic Research, 1050 Massachusettes Avenue, Cambridge, Massachusetts, 02138, U. S. A.

Dorfman, R., P. A. Samuelson, and R. M. Solow (1958), _Linear Programming and Econmomic Analysis_, New York: McGraw-Hill Book Company.

Depuit, J. (1944), "De la mesure de l'utilité des travaux publics," _Annales des Ponts et Chaussées_ 8, translated as "On the Measurement of the Utility of Public Works," _International Economic Papers_ 2, (1952), pp.83-110.

Epstein, L. G (1984), "Duality Theory and Functional Forms for Dynamic Factor Demand," _Review of Economic Studies_ 48, pp.81-95.

Epstein, L. G. (1983), "Aggregating Quasi-fixed Factors," _Scandinavian Journal of Economics_ 85, pp.191-205.

Farrell, M. J. (1957), "The Measurement of Productive Efficiency," _Journal of the Royal Statistical Society_ (Series A) 120, pp.253-281.

Fisher, F. M. (1982), "Aggregate Production Functions Revisited: The Mobility of Capital and the Rigidity of Thought," _Review of Economic Studies_ 49, pp.615-626.

Fisher, I. (1922), _The Making of Index Numbers_, Boston: Houghton Mifflin.

Fuss, M., D. McFadden, and Y. Mundlak (1978), "A Survey of Functional Forms in the Economic Analysis of Production," pp.219-268 in _Production Economics: A Dual Approach to Theory and Applications_, Vol. 1, Amsterdam: North-Holland.

Gallant, A.R., and E.H. Golub (1985), "Imposing Curvature Restrictions on Flexible Functional Forms," _Journal of Econometrics_, forthcoming.

Ginsburgh, V., and J. Waelbroeck (1981), Activity Analysis and General Equilibrium Modelling. Amsterdam: North-Holland.

Gorman, W. M. (1968), "Measuring the Quantities of Fixed Factors," pp.141-172 in Value, Capital and Growth: Papers in Honour of Sir John Hicks, J. N. Wolfe (ed.), Chicago: Aldine Publishing Co.

Green, J. E. Kohlberg, and J. Laffont (1975), "Partial Equilibrium Approach to the Free Rider Problem," Harvard Institute of Economic Research Discussion Paper 436, Harvard University, Cambridge, Massachusetts.

Griliches, Z. (1979), "Issues in Assessing the Contribution of Research and Development of Productivity Growth," Bell Journal of Economics 10, pp.92-116.

Griliches, Z. (1984), "Data Problems in Econometrics," Technical Working Paper 39, NBER, 1050 Massachusetts Avenue, Cambridge, Massachusetts, U.S.A.

Groves, T. (1976), "Information, Incentives and the Internalization of Production Externalities," pp.65-83 in Theory and Measurement of Economic Externalities, S. A. Y. Lin. (ed.) New York: Academic Press.

Harberger, A. C. (1974), Taxation and Welfare, Boston: Little, Brown and Company.

Harris, R. (1978), "On the Choice of Large Projects," Canadian Journal of Economics 11, 404-423.

Heal, G. M. (1969), "Planning without Prices," Review of Economic Studies 36, pp.347-362.

Heal, G. M. (1971), "Planning, Prices and Increasing Returns," Review of Economic Studies 38, 281-294.

Hicks, J. R. (1946), Value and Capital, Oxford: Clarendon Press.

Hirschleifer, J. (1956), "On the Economics of Transfer Pricing," Journal of Business 29, pp.172-184.

Hoffman, K. C., and D. W. Jorgenson (1972), "Economic and Technological Models for the Evaluation of Energy Policy," Bell Journal of Economics 8, pp.444-466.

Hotelling, H. (1932), "Edgeworth's Taxation Paradox and the Nature of Demand and Supply Functions," Journal of Political Economy 40, pp.577-615.

Hotelling, H. (1935), "Demand Functions with Limited Budgets," Econometrica 3, pp. 66-78.

Hotelling H. (1938), "The General Welfare in Relation to Problems of Taxation and of Railway and Utility Rates." Econometrica 6, pp.242-269.

Hulten, C. R., and F. C. Wykoff (1981), "The Measurement of Economic Depreciation," pp.81-125 in C. R. Hulten (ed.), Depreciation, Inflation and the Taxation of Income from Capital, Washington, D. C.: The Urban Institute Press.

Jorgenson, D. W. (1963), "Capital Theory and Investment Behavior," American Economic Review 53, pp.247-259.

Jorgenson, D. W. (1984a), "Econometric Methods for Applied General Equilibrium Analysis," pp.139-203 in Applied General Equilibrium Analysis, H. E. Scarf and J. B. Shoven (eds.), London: Cambridge University Press.

Jorgensen, D. W. (1984b), "Econometric Methods for Modeling Producer Behavior," Discussion Paper 1086, Harvard Institute for Economic Research, Harvard Unversity, Cambridge, Massachusetts.

Jorgenson, D. W., and B. M. Fraumeni (1981), "Relative Prices and Technical Change," pp.17-47 in Modeling and Measuring Natural Resource Substitution, E. R. Berndt and B. C. Field (eds.), Cambridge, Mass.: M.I.T. Press.

Kaizuka, K. (1965), "Public Goods and Decentralization of Production," Review of Economics and Statistics 47, 118-120.

Kanemoto, Y (1980), "A Note on the Measurement of Benefits of Public Inputs," Canadian Journal of Economics 13, 135-142.

Kanemoto, Y., and K. Mera (1984), "General Equilibrium Analysis of Large Transportation Improvements," Department of Economics, Queen's University, Kingston, Canada.

Kanemoto, Y. (1985), "Estimating Benefits of Infrastructure through the Analysis of Land Value," Department of Economics, Queen's University, Kingston, Canada.

Karlin, S. (1959), Mathematical Methods and Theory in Games, Programming and Economics, Vol. 1, Palo Alto, California: Addison-Wesley.

Khang, C. (1971), "An Isovalue Locus involving Intermediate Goods and its Applications to the Pure Theory of International Trade," Journal of International Economics 1, pp.315-325.

Kuhn, H. W., and A. W. Tucker (1951), "Nonlinear Programming," pp.481-492 in The Proceedings of the Second Berkeley Symposium on Mathetical Statistics and Probability, J. Neyman (ed.), Berkeley: University of California Press.

Kopp, R. J., and V. K. Smith (1983), "Neoclassical Modelling of Nonneutral Technological Change: An Experimental Appraisal," The Scandinavian Journal of Economics 85, pp.127-146.

Lau, L. T. (1974), "Applications of Duality Theory: Comments," pp.176-199 in Frontiers of Quantitative Economics, Vol. II, M. D. Intriligator and D. A. Kendrick (eds.), Amsterdam: North-Holland.

Lau, L. J. (1978), "Testing and Imposing Monotonicity, Convexity and Quasiconvexity Constraints," pp.409-453 in *Production Economics: A Dual Approach to Theory and Applications*, Vol. 1, M. Fuss and D. McFadden (eds.), Amsterdam: North-Holland.

Lau, L. J. (1984a), "Comments," pp.127-137 in *Applied General Equilibrium Analysis*, H. E. Scarf and J. B. Shoven (eds.), London: Cambridge University Press.

Lau, J. J. (1984b), "Functional Forms in Econometric Model Building," Department of Economics, Stanford University, Stanford, California.

Mangasarian, O. L. (1969), *Nonlinear Programming*, New York: McGraw-Hill.

Manne, A. (1977), "General Equilibrium with Activity Analysis," in *Modelling Energy-Economy Interactions: Five Approaches*, C. Hitch (ed.), Washington, DC: Resources for the Future.

Mansur, A., and J. Whalley (1984), "Numerical Specification of Applied General Equilibrium Models: Estimation, Calibration and Data," pp.69-127 in *Applied General Equilibrium Analysis*, H. E. Scarf and J. B. Shoven (eds.), London: Cambridge University Press.

Marshall, A. (1920), *Principles of Economics*, London: Macmillan.

May, K. (1946), "The Aggregation Problem for a One-Industry Model," *Econometrica* 14, pp.285-298.

McFadden, D. (1966), "Cost, Revenue and Profit Functions: A Cursory Review," Working Paper #86, IBER, University of California at Berkeley, March.

McFadden, D. (1978), "The General Linear Profit Function," pp.269-286 in *Production Economics: A Dual Approach to Theory and Applications*, Vol. 1, M. Fuss and D. McFadden (eds.), Amsterdam: North-Holland.

Mohr, M. F. (1985), "The Theory and Measurement of the Rental Price of Capital in Industry Specific Productivity Analysis," forthcoming in Studies in Productivity Analysis, Vol. 6, A. Dogramaci (ed.), Boston: Martinus Nijhoff Publishing Co.

Negishi, T. (1972), General Equilibrium Theory and International Trade, Amsterdam: North-Holland.

Russell, R. R., and R. Boyce (1974), "A Multilateral Model of Internatinal Trade Flows: A Theoretical Framework and Specification of Functional Forms," Institute for Policy Analysis, La Jolla, California.

Samuelson, P. A. (1947), Foundations of Economic Analysis, Cambridge: Harvard University Press.

Samuelson, P. A. (1953-54), "Prices of Factors and Goods in General Equilibrium," Review of Economic Studies 21, pp.1-20.

Samuelson, P. A. (1964), "Tax Deductibility of Economic Depreciation to Ensure Invariant Valuations," Journal of Political Economy 72, pp.604-606.

Sandmo, A. (1972), "Optimality Rules for the Provision of Collective Factors of Production," Journal of Public Economics, 1, pp.149-157.

Shephard, R. W. (1953), Cost and Production Functions, Princeton, N. J.: Princeton University Press.

Shephard, R. W. (1970), Theory of Cost and Production Functions, Princeton, N.J.: Princeton University Press.

Shoven, J. B., and J. Whalley (1984), "Applied General Equilibrium Models of Taxation and International Trade: An Introduction and Survey," Journal of Economic Literature 22, pp.1008-1051.

Smith, V. L. (1963), "Tax Depreciation Policy and Investment Theory," International Economic Review 4, pp.80-91.

Strang, G. (1976), Linear Algebra and Its Applications, New York: Academic Press.

Triplett, J. E. (1983) (ed.), The Measurement of Labor Cost, Studies in Income and Wealth, Vol. 44, NBER, Chicago: University of Chicago Press.

Tsuneki, A. (1984), "Public Goods Economy and Welfare," Economics 515 paper, Department of Economics, University of British Columbia, Vancouver, Canada.

Uzawa, H. (1958), "The Kuhn-Tucker Theorem in Concave Programming," pp.32-37 in Studies in Linear and Nonlinear Programming, K. J. Arrow, L. Hurwicz and H. Uzawa (eds.), Stanford: Stanford University Press.

Varian, H. R. (1978), Microeconomic Analysis, New York: W. W. Norton.

White, K.J. (1978), "A General Computer Program for Econometric Methods - Shazam," Econometrica 46, 239.

White, K. J. (1985), UBC SHAZAM. Computing Centre, University of British Columbia, Vancouver, Canada.

Wiley, D. E., W. H. Schmidt, and W. J. Bramble (1973), "Studies of a Class of Covariance Structure Models," Journal of the American Statistical Association 68, pp.317-323.

Vol. 184: R. E. Burkard and U. Derigs, Assignment and Matching Problems: Solution Methods with FORTRAN-Programs. VIII, 148 pages. 1980.

Vol. 185: C. C. von Weizsäcker, Barriers to Entry. VI, 220 pages. 1980.

Vol. 186: Ch.-L. Hwang and K. Yoon, Multiple Attribute Decision Making – Methods and Applications. A State-of-the-Art-Survey. XI, 259 pages. 1981.

Vol. 187: W. Hock, K. Schittkowski, Test Examples for Nonlinear Programming Codes. V. 178 pages. 1981.

Vol. 188: D. Bös, Economic Theory of Public Enterprise. VII, 142 pages. 1981.

Vol. 189: A. P. Lüthi, Messung wirtschaftlicher Ungleichheit. IX, 287 pages. 1981.

Vol. 190: J. N. Morse, Organizations: Multiple Agents with Multiple Criteria. Proceedings, 1980. VI, 509 pages. 1981.

Vol. 191: H. R. Sneessens, Theory and Estimation of Macroeconomic Rationing Models. VII, 138 pages. 1981.

Vol. 192: H. J. Bierens: Robust Methods and Asymptotic Theory in Nonlinear Econometrics. IX, 198 pages. 1981.

Vol. 193: J. K. Sengupta, Optimal Decisions under Uncertainty. VII, 156 pages. 1981.

Vol. 194: R. W. Shephard, Cost and Production Functions. XI, 104 pages. 1981.

Vol. 195: H. W. Ursprung, Die elementare Katastrophentheorie. Eine Darstellung aus der Sicht der Ökonomie. VII, 332 pages. 1982.

Vol. 196: M. Nermuth, Information Structures in Economics. VIII, 236 pages. 1982.

Vol. 197: Integer Programming and Related Areas. A Classified Bibliography. 1978 – 1981. Edited by R. von Randow. XIV, 338 pages. 1982.

Vol. 198: P. Zweifel, Ein ökonomisches Modell des Arztverhaltens. XIX, 392 Seiten. 1982.

Vol. 199: Evaluating Mathematical Programming Techniques. Proceedings, 1981. Edited by J.M. Mulvey. XI, 379 pages. 1982.

Vol. 200: The Resource Sector in an Open Economy. Edited by H. Siebert. IX, 161 pages. 1984.

Vol. 201: P. M. C. de Boer, Price Effects in Input-Output-Relations: A Theoretical and Empirical Study for the Netherlands 1949–1967. X, 140 pages. 1982.

Vol. 202: U. Witt, J. Perske, SMS – A Program Package for Simulation and Gaming of Stochastic Market Processes and Learning Behavior. VII, 266 pages. 1982.

Vol. 203: Compilation of Input-Output Tables. Proceedings, 1981. Edited by J. V. Skolka. VII, 307 pages. 1982.

Vol. 204: K.C. Mosler, Entscheidungsregeln bei Risiko: Multivariate stochastische Dominanz. VII, 172 Seiten. 1982.

Vol. 205: R. Ramanathan, Introduction to the Theory of Economic Growth. IX, 347 pages. 1982.

Vol. 206: M.H. Karwan, V. Lotfi, J. Telgen, and S. Zionts, Redundancy in Mathematical Programming. VII, 286 pages. 1983.

Vol. 207: Y. Fujimori, Modern Analysis of Value Theory. X, 165 pages. 1982.

Vol. 208: Econometric Decision Models. Proceedings, 1981. Edited by J. Gruber. VI, 364 pages. 1983.

Vol. 209: Essays and Surveys on Multiple Criteria Decision Making. Proceedings, 1982. Edited by P. Hansen. VII, 441 pages. 1983.

Vol. 210: Technology, Organization and Economic Structure. Edited by R. Sato and M.J. Beckmann. VIII, 195 pages. 1983.

Vol. 211: P. van den Heuvel, The Stability of a Macroeconomic System with Quantity Constraints. VII, 169 pages. 1983.

Vol. 212: R. Sato and T. Nôno, Invariance Principles and the Structure of Technology. V, 94 pages. 1983.

Vol. 213: Aspiration Levels in Bargaining and Economic Decision Making. Proceedings, 1982. Edited by R. Tietz. VIII, 406 pages. 1983.

Vol. 214: M. Faber, H. Niemes und G. Stephan, Entropie, Umweltschutz und Rohstoffverbrauch. IX, 181 Seiten. 1983.

Vol. 215: Semi-Infinite Programming and Applications. Proceedings, 1981. Edited by A.V. Fiacco and K.O. Kortanek. XI, 322 pages. 1983.

Vol. 216: H.H. Müller, Fiscal Policies in a General Equilibrium Model with Persistent Unemployment. VI, 92 pages. 1983.

Vol. 217: Ch. Grootaert, The Relation Between Final Demand and Income Distribution. XIV, 105 pages. 1983.

Vol. 218: P. van Loon, A Dynamic Theory of the Firm: Production, Finance and Investment. VII, 191 pages. 1983.

Vol. 219: E. van Damme, Refinements of the Nash Equilibrium Concept. VI, 151 pages. 1983.

Vol. 220: M. Aoki, Notes on Economic Time Series Analysis: System Theoretic Perspectives. IX, 249 pages. 1983.

Vol. 221: S. Nakamura, An Inter-Industry Translog Model of Prices and Technical Change for the West German Economy. XIV, 290 pages. 1984.

Vol. 222: P. Meier, Energy Systems Analysis for Developing Countries. VI, 344 pages. 1984.

Vol. 223: W. Trockel, Market Demand. VIII, 205 pages. 1984.

Vol. 224: M. Kiy, Ein disaggregiertes Prognosesystem für die Bundesrepublik Deutschland. XVIII, 276 Seiten. 1984.

Vol. 225: T.R. von Ungern-Sternberg, Zur Analyse von Märkten mit unvollständiger Nachfragerinformation. IX, 125 Seiten. 1984

Vol. 226: Selected Topics in Operations Research and Mathematical Economics. Proceedings, 1983. Edited by G. Hammer and D. Pallaschke. IX, 478 pages. 1984.

Vol. 227: Risk and Capital. Proceedings, 1983. Edited by G. Bamberg and K. Spremann. VII, 306 pages. 1984.

Vol. 228: Nonlinear Models of Fluctuating Growth. Proceedings, 1983. Edited by R.M. Goodwin, M. Krüger and A. Vercelli. XVII, 277 pages. 1984.

Vol. 229: Interactive Decision Analysis. Proceedings, 1983. Edited by M. Grauer and A.P. Wierzbicki. VIII, 269 pages. 1984.

Vol. 230: Macro-Economic Planning with Conflicting Goals. Proceedings, 1982. Edited by M. Despontin, P. Nijkamp and J. Spronk. VI, 297 pages. 1984.

Vol. 231: G.F. Newell, The M/M/∞ Service System with Ranked Servers in Heavy Traffic. XI, 126 pages. 1984.

Vol. 232: L. Bauwens, Bayesian Full Information Analysis of Simultaneous Equation Models Using Integration by Monte Carlo. VI, 114 pages. 1984.

Vol. 233: G. Wagenhals, The World Copper Market. XI, 190 pages. 1984.

Vol. 234: B.C. Eaves, A Course in Triangulations for Solving Equations with Deformations. III, 302 pages. 1984.

Vol. 235: Stochastic Models in Reliability Theory. Proceedings, 1984. Edited by S. Osaki and Y. Hatoyama. VII, 212 pages. 1984.

Vol. 236: G. Gandolfo, P.C. Padoan, A Disequilibrium Model of Real and Financial Accumulation in an Open Economy. VI, 172 pages. 1984.

Vol. 237: Misspecification Analysis. Proceedings, 1983. Edited by T.K. Dijkstra. V, 129 pages. 1984.

Vol. 238: W. Domschke, A. Drexl, Location and Layout Planning. IV, 134 pages. 1985.

Vol. 239: Microeconomic Models of Housing Markets. Edited by K. Stahl. VII, 197 pages. 1985.

Vol. 240: Contributions to Operations Research. Proceedings, 1984. Edited by K. Neumann and D. Pallaschke. V, 190 pages. 1985.

Vol. 241: U. Wittmann, Das Konzept rationaler Preiserwartungen. XI, 310 Seiten. 1985.

Vol. 242: Decision Making with Multiple Objectives. Proceedings, 1984. Edited by Y. Y. Haimes and V. Chankong. XI, 571 pages. 1985.

Vol. 243: Integer Programming and Related Areas. A Classified Bibliography 1981–1984. Edited by R. von Randow. XX, 386 pages. 1985.

Vol. 244: Advances in Equilibrium Theory. Proceedings, 1984. Edited by C. D. Aliprantis, O. Burkinshaw and N. J. Rothman. II, 235 pages. 1985.

Vol. 245: J. E. M. Wilhelm, Arbitrage Theory. VII, 114 pages. 1985.

Vol. 246: P. W. Otter, Dynamic Feature Space Modelling, Filtering and Self-Tuning Control of Stochastic Systems. XIV, 177 pages. 1985.

Vol. 247: Optimization and Discrete Choice in Urban Systems. Proceedings, 1983. Edited by B. G. Hutchinson, P. Nijkamp and M. Batty. VI, 371 pages. 1985.

Vol. 248: Plural Rationality and Interactive Decision Processes. Proceedings, 1984. Edited by M. Grauer, M. Thompson and A. P. Wierzbicki. VI, 354 pages. 1985.

Vol. 249: Spatial Price Equilibrium: Advances in Theory, Computation and Application. Proceedings, 1984. Edited by P. T. Harker. VII, 277 pages. 1985.

Vol. 250: M. Roubens, Ph. Vincke, Preference Modelling. VIII, 94 pages. 1985.

Vol. 251: Input-Output Modeling. Proceedings, 1984. Edited by A. Smyshlyaev. VI, 261 pages. 1985.

Vol. 252: A. Birolini, On the Use of Stochastic Processes in Modeling Reliability Problems. VI, 105 pages. 1985.

Vol. 253: C. Withagen, Economic Theory and International Trade in Natural Exhaustible Resources. VI, 172 pages. 1985.

Vol. 254: S. Müller, Arbitrage Pricing of Contingent Claims. VIII, 151 pages. 1985.

Vol. 255: Nondifferentiable Optimization: Motivations and Applications. Proceedings, 1984. Edited by V. F. Demyanov and D. Pallaschke. VI, 350 pages. 1985.

Vol. 256: Convexity and Duality in Optimization. Proceedings, 1984. Edited by J. Ponstein. V, 142 pages. 1985.

Vol. 257: Dynamics of Macrosystems. Proceedings, 1984. Edited by J.-P. Aubin, D. Saari and K. Sigmund. VI, 280 pages. 1985.

Vol. 258: H. Funke, Eine allgemeine Theorie der Polypol- und Oligopolpreisbildung. III, 237 pages. 1985.

Vol. 259: Infinite Programming. Proceedings, 1984. Edited by E. J. Anderson and A. B. Philpott. XIV, 244 pages. 1985.

Vol. 260: H.-J. Kruse, Degeneracy Graphs and the Neighbourhood Problem. VIII, 128 pages. 1986.

Vol. 261: Th. R. Gulledge, Jr., N. K. Womer, The Economics of Made-to-Order Production. VI, 134 pages. 1986.

Vol. 262: H. U. Buhl, A Neo-Classical Theory of Distribution and Wealth. V, 146 pages. 1986.

Vol. 263: M. Schäfer, Resource Extraction and Market Structure. XI, 154 pages. 1986.

Vol. 264: Models of Economic Dynamics. Proceedings, 1983. Edited by H. F. Sonnenschein. VII, 212 pages. 1986.

Vol. 265: Dynamic Games and Applications in Economics. Edited by T. Başar. IX, 288 pages. 1986.

Vol. 266: Multi-Stage Production Planning and Inventory Control. Edited by S. Axsäter, Ch. Schneeweiss and E. Silver. V, 264 pages. 1986.

Vol. 267: R. Bemelmans, The Capacity Aspect of Inventories. IX, 165 pages. 1986.

Vol. 268: V. Firchau, Information Evaluation in Capital Markets. VII, 103 pages. 1986.

Vol. 269: A. Borglin, H. Keiding, Optimality in Infinite Horizon Economies. VI, 180 pages. 1986.

Vol. 270: Technological Change, Employment and Spatial Dynamics. Proceedings 1985. Edited by P. Nijkamp. VII, 466 pages. 1986.

Vol. 271: C. Hildreth, The Cowles Commission in Chicago, 1939–1955. V, 176 pages. 1986.

Vol. 272: G. Clemenz, Credit Markets with Asymmetric Information. VIII, 212 pages. 1986.

Vol. 273: Large-Scale Modelling and Interactive Decision Analysis. Proceedings, 1985. Edited by G. Fandel, M. Grauer, A. Kurzhanski and A. P. Wierzbicki. VII, 363 pages. 1986.

Vol. 274: W. K. Klein Haneveld, Duality in Stochastic Linear and Dynamic Programming. VII, 295 pages. 1986.

Vol. 275: Competition, Instability, and Nonlinear Cycles. Proceedings, 1985. Edited by W. Semmler. XII, 340 pages. 1986.

Vol. 276: M. R. Baye, D. A. Black, Consumer Behavior, Cost of Living Measures, and the Income Tax. VII, 119 pages. 1986.

Vol. 277: Studies in Austrian Capital Theory, Investment and Time. Edited by M. Faber. VI, 317 pages. 1986.

Vol. 278: W. E. Diewert, The Measurement of the Economic Benefits of Infrastructure Services. V, 202 pages. 1986.